DORÉ DEVERELL live Angeles, California, where she lectured, taught, counselled and wrote on health-related subjects. Since moving to Sacramento and attending Rudolf Steiner College, she has worked at the local Waldorf School tutoring children in remedial reading, and also teaching Asian students English. She is currently writing about her experience of child abuse, alcoholism, cancer and suicide, and how overcoming them can be a path of spiritual development. She was born in Oklahoma in 1923 and has two children and three grandchildren.

LIGHT BEYOND THE DARKNESS

LIGHT BEYOND THE DARKNESS

THE HEALING OF A SUICIDE
ACROSS THE THRESHOLD OF DEATH

DORÉ DEVERELL

With a Foreword by
George G. Ritchie, Jr., M.D.

CLAIRVIEW
LONDON

Clairview Books
An imprint of Temple Lodge Publishing
51 Queen Caroline Street
Hammersmith, London W6 9QL

www.clairviewbooks.com

Published by Clairview 2000
Reprinted 2000

First published by Temple Lodge Publishing
London 1996

© Doré Deverell 1996

Doré Deverell asserts the moral right to
be identified as the author of this work

All rights reserved. No part of this publication may be
reproduced, stored in a retrieval system, or transmitted,
in any form or by any means, electronic, mechanical,
photocopying or otherwise, without the prior
permission of the publishers

A catalogue record for this book
is available from the British Library

ISBN 1 902636 19 8

Cover by Andrew Morgan Design
Typeset by DP Photosetting, Aylesbury, Bucks.
Printed and bound in Great Britain by
Cromwell Press Limited, Trowbridge, Wilts.

This book is dedicated to the individuality who was my son, Richard Deverell. His life and suffering brought us both onto a spiritual path, which I hope we can walk together as companions through many lifetimes.

Contents

Acknowledgements

Many people have been involved with the writing of this book. I look back over the seven years and it amazes me how each person came at the right moment with suggestions or comments that pushed the book forward another step. I experienced deeply that whatever we do, it is a community affair.

I wish to thank Marijo Rogers for her editing, suggestions and encouragement during the beginning stages of this book.

I am extremely grateful to Meg Gorman who carried this book in her consciousness despite heavy work commitments, and made suggestions for countless rewrites. Meg constantly told me that I could write it without a ghost writer's help. She also thought it was an important book which needed to be written. A young man named Jeff Barnum encouraged me to write about my feelings. Jeff also received the contents of the book with great reverence and vision. Several other friends read parts of the book and gave their suggestions. Each suggestion contributed to the book.

My gratitude to Rudolf Steiner and the light he has brought to us struggling humans is immeasurable.

Foreword

This book is the best I have ever seen for people who have suffered through having a member of their family commit suicide. It contains information that is extremely important both to the soul who committed suicide and to the loved ones left behind who wish to help. I treasure having a copy of it.

From having been on the 'other side' through my near death experience, and having had the Christ give me a glimpse of the terrible consequence of suicide motivated by negative emotions, I understand even better the courage this book took for both the author and the soul of her son Richard. Doré Deverell should be saluted for her courage, tenacity and most of all love for both herself and her son, as demonstrated through this book.

We must thank Doré for the time and effort which she has taken to bring this outstanding work into a book so that others may benefit from her experience. Thank God she was lead the way she was and thank you Christ and Richard for the results.

George G. Ritchie, Jr., MD
Author of *Return from Tomorrow* and *Ordered to Return*

Preface

My son Richard committed suicide on 11 July 1982, a few weeks before his thirty-sixth birthday. His death was a shock, but not a total surprise. His life had been unbelievably tragic.

I hadn't known how to help him during his life, though I never stopped trying. When he died I knew how to help him even less.

I knew from reading and intuition that suicide is not a release from pain. I believed he was experiencing greater anguish after his death than anything he had suffered during his life. I believed that his suicide doomed him to total isolation in the spiritual worlds, much worse than his isolation on earth. I believed he would have to endure incomprehensible remorse for ending his life.

The agony of his life and death welled up in my heart. Seeking relief of any kind, I enrolled him in perpetual prayer groups in the Catholic Church. I prayed for him constantly.

Richard's death brought forth with full force many questions. Why had he suffered so? Could another mother have helped him more? Did my problems cause his? Why hadn't we found the proper help for him? Why had all segments of our culture failed him?

I felt I had failed Richard as his mother.

Religion failed Richard. We were Catholics. I went to daily mass. I didn't find there anything that helped explain Richard's life.

Medicine failed Richard. The doctors treated his epilepsy by giving him drugs whose side-effects robbed him of the quality of life and the ability to contact his higher self for guidance. I know what drugs can do. I lost seven years of my life by taking prescribed drugs from a psychiatrist.

Education failed Richard. His degree in Political Science didn't enable him to support himself.

Government institutions failed Richard. The Social Security Administration provided him with minimal subsistence through SSI. However, their programmes couldn't habilitate or rehabilitate him.

I didn't blame any of the above, except myself. All of them had tried. None of us had the solutions.

When I received some money from Richard's share of his father's estate, I vowed to use the money to help others like Richard. To do that I first had to find the knowledge. I didn't know how or where, but I would! I couldn't bear to believe that Richard's life had been meaningless.

In my search for answers, I learned that I could help Richard by reading spiritually inspired works to him. I started immediately. I read daily, and, to my amazement, things began to change for both of us.

After several years of reading, I wanted to share my experience with others. However, when I started to write about Richard's life, I frequently had to put the book aside. I had to face the tragedy of his life. I had to face my failure as his mother. I had to face the darkness that had enveloped both of our souls. Not until we both had found some light could I bear to look back on that darkness. Finally, I could finish the book.

The book tells about my journey into unchartered territory and the transformation of my son's life after death. Along the way, I found answers to many of the burning questions mentioned above.

I learned why I hadn't found help for Richard. I had been looking in the wrong places. I discovered that answers could only be found in the spiritual worlds through meditation. I found medical doctors, psychiatrists, priests, teachers, group homes, musicians and spiritual scientists who could have helped Richard, in spite of his difficulties, to live a meaningful life. All of these individuals were meditants on a spiritual path, bringing their spiritual research into their work.

I know that I still have only a thimbleful of understanding, but I want to share my experience with you for several reasons. Suicide is becoming rampant throughout the world, especially in the age group 15 to 25. I have come to see that death is never a release from suffering, and that suicide is never a viable choice. Suicide is a profound tragedy with dire consequences. I hope my findings will help deter others from committing suicide.

However, if you have lost children, spouses, family, or friends to suicide, you can help them and yourself. Perhaps my discoveries will bring you release from pain.

Finally, I want to share my unspeakable joy with you. I experienced by persevering on a spiritual path, by continuing to read to Richard, that he was able to return quickly to a new life on earth. His soul is filled with more light this time. He has beautiful, loving, light-filled parents. Possibly my experience will bring you renewed hope.

Oh, the ineffable joy of it! To apprehend that no darkness can withstand spiritual light forever. To experience that regardless of the depth to which one falls spiritual striving can lift one to the heights. To perceive that death of the body is not the end. To see that even suicide can be transformed.

I hope you will join me on this journey, which begins in deepest darkness and haltingly becomes a path to the light.

Doré Deverell
Carmichael, California
15 January 1996

Doré can be contacted at:
PO Box 2045, Fair Oaks, CA 95628, USA
e-mail: dore@macnexus.org
web-site: www.waldorfshop.net/lightbeyond

Part I

RICHARD'S LIFE AND DEATH

1
The Beginning—1946

The moment I saw my new-born son, Richard, filled me with anxiety about being a mother. Words of my father returned to me as I saw his tiny body: 'I can't imagine your being a mother.'

My impoverished and abuse-filled childhood had not prepared me for motherhood. At home with the baby, I felt an abyss between myself and him. When I tried to cuddle, he would draw away and whimper. Intuitively, I felt something was wrong.

As he grew, he became increasingly inward, playing alone endlessly with his blocks and toys without noticing me. I told my husband, Clyde, 'I feel so unnecessary to Richard except for meeting his physical needs.'

'How can you say that about a little baby?' he asked.

Richard talked very little, so I began reading an alphabet book to him when he was about two and a half. He learned very quickly to read the letters to me.

Hoping he would connect with other children, I started to work and put Richard in nursery school, but he didn't connect. I felt better working, but I felt so guilty at leaving Richard that I quit working when he was four. A child psychologist assured me at that time that Richard wasn't mentally retarded. Since he was so unresponsive emotionally, however, I was sure I had failed him as a mother.

On the other hand, Richard showed great abilities of learning; for example, he learned to ride a bicycle in a number of weeks at age four.

One day when Richard was five, he said to me, 'Mommy, I want you to call me Richard. I don't like being called Dickie.'

I tried to comply, but kept forgetting. He then began to call me Dottie, a nickname Clyde had given me. When I asked him to call me Mommy, he said he would do so when I called him Richard. I made the extra effort and finally succeeded. As promised, he once again called me Mommy.

I felt bemused at this entire interchange. Was it healthy for a five-year-old to so cleverly manipulate his mother? He didn't seem like a child to me but more like a calculating adult. I couldn't understand where he'd learned to think like that.

Though intelligent beyond his years in some ways, his inwardness invited other children to abuse him. He quickly became the neighbourhood scapegoat. Living in surburbia in Los Angeles was my first opportunity of observing Richard with other children in an unstructured situation. Watching the children pushing him around churned chaotic feelings in me. I felt helpless in these situations. To comfort myself at such times, I told myself, 'Richard will find friends of like intelligence when he starts school.'

Truthfully, since I could remember, school was the only place I had found any connections to life. I loved the learning, but I still had a deep soul thirst which I wasn't able to quench. No one else seemed to feel like this. I couldn't articulate this yearning, but when I was 16, growing up in the Bible Belt in Oklahoma, I called on a minister and asked: 'What can I do for God?'

He looked at me in surprise, 'You can tithe 10% of your money to Him,' he answered. That wasn't much help.

By age 18 I moved to California by myself and worked as a secretary until my marriage. It was wonderful to be the darling of the executives and salesmen, but this yearning didn't abate. When I was 20 I wrote:

On Reading T.S. Eliot

For years I did implore it
Then decided to ignore it,

And did pretty well at that.
At least, it was a brave pretence
Of grasping cold and common sense
To create a habitat.
One to touch the earth and dwell there,
To accept heaven and hell there.
Others seemed to live it
With their mechanical routine
And occasionally different scene
Of action to give it.
Unmindful of the other plane
That constantly usurped my brain
Yet could not be expressed.

But at last I saw it written
By some other thusly smitten
All of it I had repressed.
So, around it I shall build my own hearth
And only when compelled, shall I touch earth.

I look back on this poem 50 years later and I'm amazed that I knew other planes existed. Nothing in my background or education had told me so.

The next year I married, hoping to find fulfilment for these yearnings. Marriage was not the answer. I felt more unfulfilled than ever and agonized at my feelings of complete inadequacy as a mother.

2
School Years

When Richard was five, and we moved near the beach, we had another son, David. I was much more relaxed with David, who was an affectionate and responsive child. By the time David could walk, he wouldn't leave home without his little blue, rubber teddy bear. To my surprise, Richard, who was six, for the first time began to bring his teddy bear along, too. I wondered if Richard was trying to connect with something in imitating David.

I was glad to leave the old neighbourhood and hoped that Richard would make friends and find his intellectual peers by attending American Martyrs parochial school.

Richard continued to show a logical mind. In a moment of intense need, after a particularly heated argument between Clyde and me one day, I impulsively asked Richard whom he would rather live with if his father and I were separated.

He thought for a moment, then said, 'I would rather live with both of you. If I have to choose, I would choose Daddy.' I was crushed.

Since Clyde was on a business trip, Richard later asked: 'You are unhappy with Daddy being gone, aren't you?'

'Yes,' I replied.

In a most reasonable voice Richard asked, 'Then, how do you think you would feel if he were gone all of the time?'

I remember the conversation so clearly to this day. Though Richard was only six, his answer was so adult it jolted me.

During Richard's grammar school years, he continued to be a loner and was rejected by many of his teachers, too, except during his third grade. That year he finally had a friend for the entire year and they got along perfectly. To my dismay, this friend moved away at the end of the year.

I enrolled him in many sports outside school. He failed at each one.

Meanwhile, I was having my own social problems. I joined the mother's club at Richard's school. When I wasn't asked to run for president after serving a term as treasurer, I was disappointed. At the couples club parties alcohol made me too friendly; some of the women thought I was flirting with their husbands!

Withdrawing from the mother's club, I started searching for help in earnest. I hungrily began reading Catholic literature. For many years I read voraciously, and identified with the dark night of the soul of the saints. I found a layman's version of St Thomas Aquinas' *Summa Theologica* titled *My Way of Life*. The opening grabbed my attention immediately. I avidly read the entire book, feeling intensely alive and full of passion throughout. I tried sharing my reading with my husband, Clyde. He wasn't interested.

'What do you want out of life?' I asked.

'Don't most people live a life of quiet desperation,' he answered.

'Not me. I'm not going to settle for that,' I vowed.

I couldn't find anyone to share my searching. A study group that I had initiated with a local priest ended after a few months, but I continued to read in solitude and pain.

About this time I met Gerry, an Irish woman with six children, two of whom were boys the same as my two. Her son Patrick, who was the same age as Richard, had similar problems. Patrick was her fourth child within nine years, and there was always a lot going on in the Connell house. Gerry was very easy going, and we became best friends. She accepted life as it came, did the best she could and moved on to the next challenge.

What a blessing it was for me and my boys to know Gerry and her family. The boys and I practically lived at the

Connell house. It was such a relief for me to have a place to go where Richard was totally accepted. With Gerry's loving acceptance, I learned to relax more with the boys and to give them more freedom.

These relationships between the two families continued for several years. Although Richard never had another friend during these years, he could interact with the Connells.

When Richard was ten, I finally found something for him. He began to learn to play the piano, which he enjoyed immensely. He liked to practise and I felt at last he had found his niche. His isolation didn't seem as bad to me since he had the piano. Weren't artists different from other people? I was sure when he got to college and continued his music that he would find people to whom he could relate.

By the summer that Richard was 12 he had progressed rapidly and had become one of the better pianists at recitals. He loved to listen to classical music.

One day he approached me, 'I would like to start composing music. Could you find me a teacher?'

'That's wonderful,' I responded. 'I'll find one and you can begin.'

Richard really enjoyed these lessons. Within a few months he composed a complicated piece that required months of practice before he could play it well.

Richard's piano teacher arranged an afternoon recital just for him to present his composition. As I watched Richard playing the piano dressed formally in a black tailored suit with tie, my heart swelled with pride and gratitude. You could have heard a pin drop during his presentation and the audience enthusiastically applauded. I had been right all along. His music would help him make a life.

Richard's life at school, however, was still miserable. He was rejected by the children and was the bane of his teachers' existence. He lived in his own little world.

When he was in eighth grade, I was at the school one day

on business and I happened to walk by his classroom and glanced in. There was Richard sitting on a stool in front of the room with a dunce hat on his head! I immediately went into the principal and asked if Richard couldn't be spared such humiliation. The nun sat there with her hands folded in front of her on the desk and said: 'I can't interfere with the teacher's discipline.'

I was furious. When Richard came home I asked him what had happened. He said the nun became angry at him because he wasn't listening.

In his bemused fashion he said, 'I've been there for two days already. I have to stay there until the end of the week. It's not so bad, really, I've gotten used to it.'

Well, I'd never get used to it. I called the nun that evening. 'I think you are causing Richard great harm by making him wear that dunce hat all week. Since your principal won't intervene, I request that you let Richard play the piano at an assembly for his eighth grade class.' She agreed.

A friend who had a son in the class told me her son said, 'He really played.' Richard's teacher was amazed. She said she had no idea that Richard was so talented. 'Everyone has something,' she added, as if she had given up trying to find Richard's something.

In the yearbook of his eighth grade graduation class, they predicted that Richard would be a great composer.

Richard seemed content with his music and resigned to having no friends. Since he was always at home, we spent much time together. We would talk about his future and his composing. He began to read biographies of classical composers. Richard and I were very close in some ways. We painted fences and did other chores together. I was his only companion really. My husband remarked once that I was like a lion with its cub.

Richard's grammar school years were over. I was sure that high school would offer him more opportunities for friends. David had finished third grade. Clyde had finally completed his Master's degree in Electronic Engineering. However, all was not well. A nightly ritual of wine before dinner had begun.

3
High School Years

An ominous event occurred in the summer after Richard's uneventful first year of high school. The family had returned late the night before from an extremely stressful camping trip in the high Sierras. I was in the kitchen getting a cup of coffee when Clyde yelled for me in a panic-stricken voice. I rushed into the living room to find Richard lying on the floor, writhing and foaming at the mouth.

'He made a noise and fell on the floor,' Clyde said, wringing his hands. 'It looks like he's having an epileptic seizure.'

I couldn't bear the thought. Kneeling down beside him, I patted his head, feeling desperate and helpless. 'Call Dr Johnson, ask him what we should do,' I screamed at Clyde in utter panic. Seeing a seizure first hand terrified me. I had never wanted to be near anyone having a seizure.

Putting down the phone, Clyde said, 'Doctor Johnson wants to put Richard in the hospital for tests. He'll meet us there this afternoon. Meanwhile, if he has another seizure, we are to use a spoon to prevent Richard from biting his tongue.'

Clyde kept his composure as always, for which I was grateful. I don't know how he felt inside.

Richard had stopped jerking and now lay still with his eyes closed. When he opened them, he looked around him in confusion. 'What happened?' he asked.

'You had a seizure,' his father answered. 'We're taking you to the hospital this afternoon. We'll know more after you have some tests.'

Richard got up off the floor and stood there woozily.

When I went to take a bath, I didn't know I was moaning

until Clyde came in. 'Don't you fall apart,' he chastised me. 'We have to stay calm. One ill person in the family is enough.'

Gloom enveloped me. If Richard had epilepsy, his rejection would increase even if he could play the piano.

The doctor found no pathology that could have caused the seizure. He prescribed phenobarbital which depressed Richard. He wouldn't get out of bed in the mornings. He wouldn't practise the piano. He became lifeless. I was frantic.

Shortly after Richard's seizure, Clyde and I began to drink wine after dinner as well as before dinner. The days with Richard were so difficult, I eagerly looked forward to wine time when Clyde came home.

Six weeks after the first seizure, Richard had another. After he recovered he asked me, 'Do you think God still wants me to be a composer?' He looked so frail, so bewildered, I could hardly bear to look at him.

'Epilepsy shouldn't stop you from composing music,' I answered, trying to reassure myself as well.

It was all too obvious that the medication had robbed Richard of interest in music or anything else. In addition, it hadn't prevented the second seizure, which frightened both of us. How could he have a life if he never knew when a seizure would knock him out? Worse than the seizures, it seemed to me that without his music he had no possibility of a life at all.

Having become isolated and obsessed with Richard, I was delighted when a friend from my days in the mother's club, Merry, asked me to go to Marymount College with her after Christmas. I clutched the idea like a drowning person.

Though Clyde couldn't understand why I needed to go to college, I went anyway. I enjoyed every minute. It was such a relief to have something to think about besides Richard.

Meanwhile, after the second seizure, I found Dr Putnam, who had dedicated his life to helping people with epilepsy.

When we arrived at his office, I felt immediate rapport with him. His deep blue eyes showed genuine compassion and undivided interest in Richard. When he asked Richard how he was feeling, Richard replied, 'I just don't feel like doing anything any more.'

'What medication have you been taking?' the doctor asked.

'Phenobarbital,' Richard answered.

'Phenobarbital is a depressant. I have discovered Dilantin which doesn't have that side-effect. I think you will feel much better off the phenobarbital.'

'I hope so,' Richard said.

'It's important for you to be as active as possible. Riding your bicycle to school is excellent. Follow my diet suggestions and we should be able to control the seizures.'

I was happy with Dr Putnam's suggestions. I had been afraid for Richard to do much of anything away from home for fear of his having a seizure in an unprotected place.

Richard felt better with Dr Putnam's directives, but he still did not return to his music. Instead, he began to talk a lot about Kit, a girl in his sophomore class.

'Have you ever spoken to her?' I asked. He would look sheepish and say, 'No.'

His interest in Kit continued for some time, but he never was able to approach her. He seemed to have lost all interest in his music which formerly had given his life meaning.

Richard's personality continued to worsen after the seizures. He refused to help around the house and his room became a disaster. I was forced to cancel his music lessons because he wouldn't do his assignments or practice.

Although I was enjoying my college classes, I dreaded the coming summer when Richard and I would be out of school. I felt more agitated about Richard's situation daily. Right before school ended, I went to a psychiatrist who prescribed anti-depressants for me. He threatened to admit me to a hospital if I refused to take them. I felt defeated, helpless and despairing.

Richard and I were completely isolated that summer. He spent the entire summer making maps showing the growth of the United States. He started with the 13 colonies and made a new map for every change during the years until the 48 states were complete. With every change, Richard would come out of his room and eagerly tell me the historic events that had culminated in the change. He stayed in his room most of the time. He had absolutely no activity outside the home during school holidays or vacations.

I continued my ardent reading of Catholic literature. I responded deeply to every word written in *That Man is You* by Abbé Louis Evely. In the chapter 'God is Love', he writes,

Our Lord expected the utmost from everyone.
Behind men's grumpiest poses
    and most puzzling defence mechanisms—
    respectability and seriousness,
    arrogance, dignified airs or coarseness,
    silence or cursing—
He could see a child
    who hadn't been loved enough
    and who'd stopped developing
    because someone'd ceased believing in him...
Inside of every human being
    God exists and wants to be detected
    so that He may thrive.

I sobbed that I had never been loved or been able to love like that. I couldn't share these feelings with anyone.

That summer I was grateful that David was away from the depressed atmosphere of the house. He attended the Junior Lifeguard programme at the beach, and played Little League baseball. Richard and I attended every game.

My greatest fear was that Richard would never be able to support himself financially. I wanted to get a degree to expand my life and to augment our income. Truthfully, I wanted a degree so I could be free to leave the marriage when both boys were through college.

After that interminable summer, I returned to Marymount in the fall and Richard started his Junior year. By spring I learned that I was pregnant again.

Knowing that I would have little free time when the baby came, I thought Richard should get a driver's licence. To my dismay, Richard wasn't eager to learn to drive. However, he did get his licence, only to lose it a few months later by having another seizure. Richard couldn't apply for another licence until he had been seizure-free for two years.

Because the Dilantin had not prevented Richard from having another seizure, I changed doctors again. Dr Walley prescribed Diamox and Mysoline, which controlled the seizures but, as I learned years later, had terrible side-effects which the doctor hadn't explained. I should have realized this myself by the Doctor's instructions: 'Watch Richard carefully as you increase the dosage. When he starts to stagger, decrease the dosage by one tablet.'

The tension of regulating the correct dosage of Richard's medication took a toll on both of us. One day, when we finally got it regulated, I asked Richard, 'Would you like to go to camp up in the high Sierra?'

To my delight Richard's eyes lit up and he said, 'Yes.' He was gone for a week, and it was such a relief to have him out of the house and doing something he liked. When he came home, his face looked relaxed and refreshed.

'Tell me what you did at the camp.'

'I spent most of the time in the woods by myself. I love the trees. I also really enjoyed listening to the forest ranger, and I followed him around a lot. Do you think it is possible for me to be a forest ranger?'

What a happy thought! 'I'll find out,' I promised.

Could this be the answer we'd been looking for? Our hopes were short-lived. The position wasn't open to anyone who had epilepsy, controlled or not. This was a bitter blow. 'I'm sure you'll find something when you go to college,' I said to encourage him.

My daughter, Ann, was born the summer Richard was 17 and David was 12. I didn't realize how much time Richard had demanded until after Ann was born.

Because of my lack of time Richard was alone a lot, and his condition worsened. In desperation I took him to the psychiatrist. He said Richard was depressed. Since he couldn't give him anti-depressants because of his epilepsy, he suggested we find someone to hire Richard to work even if we had to pay his salary. Though I tried hard, I wasn't able to do this. The doctor had no other suggestion.

With Ann's birth, my college plans went out the window. Despair engulfed me. One day I called my sister, Sue.

'Please, come over and help me make arrangements to enter a mental institution. I can't go on. I think my children would be better off without me.'

When she arrived, we talked for a while. She had had no idea that I was in such bad shape. As we talked, I said, in a moment of inspiration, 'God gave me these children. Surely, he will give me the strength to take care of them.'

So, I carried on somehow. Every night when I went to bed I'd say, 'Dear God, let me lay my head on your lap while I sleep.'

4
College Years

Meanwhile, Richard was becoming increasingly unco-operative and belligerent. He started to look unkempt. I began to feel embarrassed at his appearance.

'Please, comb your hair,' I'd say.

He'd sidle past me and ignore my request. He had begun his first year at Loyola University and was boarding there during the week. It was such a relief to have him out of the house. However, on weekends when he came home the tension would rise again.

Shortly after the semester started, Richard had a seizure in class and lost his second driver's licence.

'Why do you think you had the seizure?' I asked.

'I feel better without the medication. I wanted to see if I could do without it. I won't do that again.'

'Don't you realize what you've done? You've lost your driver's license for another two years at least, if not for the rest of your life!'

He looked down and wouldn't face me. 'I won't do that again,' he promised.

I felt trapped. We were building a bigger home on Palos Verdes Peninsula, an isolated community with no public transportation, and now Richard couldn't drive. How would he get to school?

When we moved, Richard's decline accelerated. He became very ill, with his temperature reaching 105 degrees. Dr Walley put him in the hospital immediately.

Later, Dr Walley called: 'Richard has double pneumonia and will be hospitalized for several days. He won't be able to finish this semester; he needs to regain his strength.'

How could Richard spend his time if he weren't in school?

When I talked with Dr Walley later, he told me that he wanted to put Richard in a group home for a while.

'He is so depressed. I'm afraid he might commit suicide. I know a place in Long Beach. He could move about freely there with public transportation. He could stay there until he's able to return to college. Dr Shaw, a psychiatrist, holds therapy sessions three times a week. Between the two of us, I think we can pull Richard out of this.'

'I've never thought of his committing suicide,' I said. 'Whatever you say, we'll do.'

The drive home was dark and dreary. Our move to our new home was a nightmare. The community offered no outlets for Richard.

To save my sanity, I had initiated another study group with Monsignor McCarthy. Since I couldn't resume college, I enrolled in a writing course by correspondence. We had also joined a neighbourhood couples group where alcohol was in great supply. I was still taking drugs from the psychiatrist and imbibing my nightly wine with Clyde.

Richard's stay in the group home gave him an opportunity to be on his own in a safe environment. I took comfort in Richard's activities while there. He read voraciously: philosophy, psychology, biographies. He started reading the newspaper, taking an interest in politics, and writing letters to the editor. He was much livelier. Still he kept pretty much to himself.

When I'd bring him home for a weekend, Richard would eagerly discuss the current book he was reading. Once we both read a best seller. I don't recall the name. The book had many thoughts which opposed the establishment. Richard asked me what I thought of this book. I said I thought the author had some very valid points, though I didn't agree with everything.

Richard looked pleased. 'Then you don't condemn

everything he writes because you don't agree with some?' he asked.

'Of course not,' I answered.

In the fall, Richard entered Long Beach State University and lived in a dormitory.

* * *

Meanwhile, Clyde's and my twenty-fifth wedding anniversary was fast approaching in the summer of 1969. I tried to garner enthusiasm and give a party, but my heart wasn't in it.

During a rare moment of facing reality, I had to admit there was nothing to celebrate. The marriage was miserable. Clyde and I were as different as two people could be. We couldn't communicate; we didn't agree on how to raise the children. Neither of us were able to support what the other thought or did. Richard was floundering in college. David was being exposed to drugs which began to flood the high schools. Ann was taking Ritalin for hyperactivity. I was drinking daily and taking drugs from the psychiatrist.

I couldn't pretend in front of guests that we were the happy couple celebrating 25 years of marriage. Within days I entered an alcoholic recovery programme, and threw the drugs from the psychiatrist away.

As time passed free of drugs and alcohol, I was shocked to confront the reality of Richard's condition and the devastating effects of my absorption with alcohol and him. I deplored what my drinking and prescription drugs had done to me and to my family. Slowly I began to take hold of my life.

Gradually I began to face the many problems in my family. I took Ann off Ritalin. I told David: 'My daily drinking and, especially, the prescription drugs I took robbed me of any capability of living a normal life. If you ever have a problem with drugs or alcohol, there are 12-step programmes to help you, too.'

Richard lived in dormitories for the rest of his college years and was only home for holidays and summers. However, he was never able to keep a room-mate, and he appeared more dishevelled with passing time.

His pattern of disaster continued. He had a seizure, hit his jaw on a sink, and broke several teeth. This required months of reconstruction work. Later he rode his bicycle into a moving car, breaking his nose and ankle.

In June 1970 Richard finally graduated, and there was nothing to do but to bring him home. I was apprehensive about this. I managed to find him a couple of piano students in the neighbourhood, but that quickly ended. He turned 24 in September.

After he returned, I became his scapegoat, the object on which he vented his frustration. He quickly deteriorated when he lost his independence, and I was afraid he would become suicidal again. I also knew that he couldn't live at home, yet we couldn't afford to support him outside the home any longer. I thought of one solution and approached Clyde.

'We can't go on like this. I think Richard should apply for disability. He needs to have his own space, and so do we. It seems obvious that he will never be able to work. Perhaps the state programmes can habilitate him and find work of some kind. He's an adult and won't listen to us. We don't know what to do anyway.

Clyde flinched. 'No son of mine is going on disability,' he said with finality. 'If he has to live with us the rest of his life, so be it.'

'I don't think he or we could survive having to live together. He could become suicidal again with nothing to do. You aren't the one living with him. You're either at work or in your own little world,' I fumed. 'And your glass of wine deadens the pain for you. I don't have any pain killer available to me.'

Our argument reached its usual impasse.

Indeed, the tension between Clyde and me had taken a quantum leap since I'd joined the recovery programme. He didn't want me to go to the meetings and wanted me to take drugs again. How could I have lived for 25 years with a person who didn't support me when I was trying so earnestly to save myself and our family?

In desperation, I cajoled Clyde into consulting Monsignor McCarthy who praised the recovery programme, likening it to the early Christian communities. The priest also recommended our finding some way for Richard to live on his own.

'Life should not be an endurance contest,' Monsignor said. The priest had correctly described our marriage.

Clyde didn't agree with anything Monsignor suggested. Later, when I talked with Monsignor alone he advised me to take Ann out of the situation. 'Clyde will change his mind when the full responsibility falls on him,' he predicted.

5
Richard and I Break Away

Still, I held on, although deep down I knew I couldn't go on living like this. I escaped the house every night to attend meetings. There I finally found a support group where I received unconditional love and encouragement for the first time in my life. I was aghast at the situation of my life, one of living through others and never being in touch with myself.

I finally found the courage to move out in July 1971, and Richard left a few months later, as soon as he was awarded disability. The priest's prediction had been correct. Clyde didn't like the responsibility by himself.

I didn't abandon Richard. I was fighting for my own survival. By this time I had a health crisis of my own. I had suspected for some time that I had cancer, but at that time I still wasn't willing to find out for sure. I hoped that my being out of the marriage and building my own life would turn my health around. I had seen my best friend endure agonies of treatment and die of cancer despite the treatment. I believed that she would have lived longer and more comfortably without the horrible treatments. Because of this I was more afraid of the treatment of cancer than I was of the cancer itself. Still the cancer symptoms increased.

I saw Richard occasionally. I tried to help him from time to time. I was still hounded by guilt and an unrelenting desire to see him better. I realized from my own experience how being on 'prescribed' drugs can affect one's ability to think clearly.

I finally consulted a physician's desk reference regarding Richard's medications and the side-effects. I was horrified by what I learned. Mysoline, which is a brand of primidone, was the anticonvulsant that Richard was taking: 250 milligrams twice a day. The side-effects of Mysoline are nausea, anorexia, vomiting, fatigue, hyper-irritability, emotional disturbances, sexual impotence, diplopia nystagmus (inability to focus), drowsiness, skin eruptions and possible anaemia. The other drug he used, Diamox, which is also prescribed as a diuretic, had the following adverse reactions: tingling feeling in extremities, loss of appetite, polyuria (voiding little urine at a time), drowsiness and confusion. Imagine trying to cope with life feeling like that! He'd been on 'prescribed' drugs since he was 15, and had probably forgotten what it felt like to be free of them. My heart ached for his suffering.

I felt terrible that I hadn't researched the side-effects instead of taking the doctor's word for them. I wanted to help Richard find medication that wouldn't impair his functions so much. Through a little research, I learned about orthomolecular treatment for epilepsy, which consisted of taking massive doses of certain vitamins, along with anticonvulsant medications. I asked Richard if he would be willing to see an orthomolecular psychiatrist. He agreed.

During the 40-mile drive to the doctor's office we had a chance to talk. The day was sunny and beautiful, typical for southern California. I looked at Richard closely as he settled down in the seat. He seemed more at peace, but he didn't look well. I noticed white, scaly patches on his hands. 'What's that on your hands?' I asked. He said that he was bothered with psoriasis. 'Nothing seems to alleviate it,' he told me.

'I hope this doctor can help with that, too,' I enthused. 'I discovered in the PDR that Diamox may cause skin eruptions along with many other unpleasant side-effects. This psychiatrist has helped many people with mega-vitamins.'

'Let's hope he can help me,' he replied, but without much confidence.

'What do you do with your time?' I asked.

He told me that he had rented a piano and was taking some music classes at a junior college.

'That's great,' I exclaimed.

'I'm learning to budget my money, too,' he went on. He straightened up in the seat and his voice became more lively. 'I've learned how to fix very economical meals. I found these shoes for $3.00 at a thrift store. I joined a bicycle club and I take long bike rides. I rode to Santa Barbara and came back by train. Right now I'm reading the Bible to see for myself what it means to me.'

I was impressed and happy that he was spending his time so constructively. Still, he had no friends. I tried to imagine what it would be like to have no relationships with other human beings—indeed, to have no contacts except in impersonal groups, to have no place to belong. It seemed to me that he was making the best of an unbearable situation.

The doctor welcomed us into his office. His eyes were kind and sparkled with lively intelligence. As he was talking with Richard, I was admiring his office which was decorated in warm, soft colours. On one wall hung a plaque with Rudyard Kipling's 'If'. I liked this man immediately.

The doctor was saying, 'I can't believe that any doctor would prescribe Diamox indefinitely without also protecting you with vitamins to counteract the effects. We will eliminate that drug gradually and prescribe maximum dosages of vitamins and minerals to replenish your depleted system. We will continue with the other drug until we have you stabilized. Then we will gradually replace that drug also with one not so toxic. For your general health you must do this.'

He handed Richard a set of instructions and several bottles of vitamins, and we left.

The next time I was with Richard I asked how he was feeling. 'Did the vitamin therapy make you feel better? Have you eliminated the Diamox yet?'

'I stopped taking the Diamox, but then I started having a

few petit mals, and I was afraid I'd have another seizure. I stopped taking the vitamins instead,' he replied.

'You mean you are still taking that diuretic?' I asked in disbelief. 'Yes,' he said. My heart sank. I knew the dire consequences of continuing on such a regimen, but I wasn't able to convince Richard.

Shortly before Christmas 1972, Clyde called to tell me that Richard had been badly burned. That winter had been unusually cold, and Richard's shirt had caught on fire as he was standing over a gas heater in his apartment. His arms were so badly burned that his doctors didn't know if he would have full use of them again.

'The accident happened several weeks ago, but Richard didn't call me. I found out because I have been calling him for days to invite him for Christmas. He had been released from the hospital the day I finally reached him,' Clyde concluded.

I thought I was going to pass out. 'How is he now? Have you seen him? When can I see him?' I asked.

'I'm bringing him home this evening, but Richard expressly told me that he didn't want to see or talk with you. I think you should respect his wishes,' my ex-husband advised.

I screamed at Clyde, 'Don't you ever call me again with such news when I can't do anything about it,' I shouted. I hung up the phone and immediately called my therapist. She helped me calm down and accept once again that I'm not in control; God is. All I could do was turn Richard over to God and continue to build my new life on the shambles of the past. Still it seemed that Richard was still using me as the scapegoat. His hostility towards me, coupled with the vision of his clothes being on fire, over-whelmed me.

I went to many Twelve-step meetings, talked with many friends, and prayed constantly. I had no other choice. I did send him a cheque for $500.00 which I could ill afford. But I felt I had to do something. Richard never acknowledged receiving the cheque. I had to ask his father if he had received it.

6

Letting Richard Go—Overcoming Cancer

A couple of years passed. I didn't see Richard during that time. I had had more symptoms and realized that I had to confront the cancer. It wasn't going to go away by merely starting a new life.

By this time I had taken many healing classes and had researched alternative cancer treatments. Through this I found doctors and healers who diagnosed the cancer and guided me in alternative ways to heal it, which I did without surgery, radiation or chemotherapy. I had done nothing for the past year but build a new life-style around the treatments and write a book about my experiences. I also wrote articles, but only *The Mother Earth News* published one.

Clyde continued to invite Richard for an occasional weekend and he supplied me with information about Richard. Our son had recovered completely from the burns and had remarked to his father, 'I was afraid I'd catch on fire if I opened my shirt one more time over that heater.'

Since I'd left Clyde we were friendly on the surface. He was dependable, as always, in paying alimony and child support. He loved his children and would always provide for them. I was very grateful for Clyde's financial support. I couldn't have overcome the cancer if I'd had to work for a living at that time.

I had come to see that Clyde had been like the rock of Gibraltar to me and I couldn't have survived without him. My alimony ended after five years, but Clyde worked out a way through saving himself income taxes where he was able to continue to pay me almost half of the alimony. He did so until he died three years later.

It was only after a few more years that I realized that the real reason I left Clyde wasn't just the conflict in our marriage, but that the time had come when my destiny led me in a new direction away from him. Our lives had become completely incompatible. Clyde never dated after our divorce, but I started dating the year after.

The next time I heard from Richard was on the morning of my birthday in August 1976. I had just begun my writing for the day when the phone rang. To my surprise it was Richard.

'I want to wish you a happy birthday,' he said. 'I was just going to bed. I've been up all night. I know that's not a good way to live, but I can't seem to help it.'

'I'm so happy you called,' I said. 'Could you come out and spend the weekend? I'd like to hear what you've been doing, and I have a lot to tell you about what I've been involved in the past couple of years. I'd like to share some of the new philosophies I've found in my search.'

We made a date and hung up. I was so touched that he not only had remembered my birthday but had called also. He had never, up to that time, acknowledged my birthday. I had never received a gift from him or a card. Before he came, I gathered a lot of discarded clothes from my boyfriend to give him.

I looked forward to the weekend with mixed emotions. I dreaded to see how he looked, but I was also eager to see him. When he walked in the door, I saw that his clothes looked dingy, not too clean. I noticed that his hands were still white and scaly. His manner was reticent with me as if I were a stranger. He looked emaciated, and his colour was unhealthy.

'I have tickets for a concert,' I said. Both Rachmaninov and Tchaikovsky are on the programme.'

Richard smiled. 'I've been playing Liszt lately. I read his biography, too. I feel I can understand his music better when I read about him.'

'I'm glad you've returned to your music,' I said.

I also played a triangle in the South Bay Symphony for a while. That is, I did until the day I dropped it in the middle of the performance.' He looked sheepish when he said this as if to imply, 'Why did I ever think I could do anything right?'

'That's too bad,' I commiserated.

To change the subject, I told him I had a lot of clothes for him. 'My boyfriend, John, doesn't need them any more. Would you like to try them on and choose those you like?'

His eyes brightened. He seemed to enjoy donning the clothes which fit him fairly well. 'I think I'll wear this jacket to the concert tonight,' he said.

'What else have you been doing?' I asked.

'I've been taking speech classes, and I've joined the Toastmaster's Club. I haven't given any speeches yet, but I enjoy listening to the others. I write letters to the editors of the Los Angeles Times. I'm reading the Bible for the second time. Maybe I missed something the first time.'

I shared with him that I had just completed a book titled *How I Healed My Cancer Holistically* which hadn't yet been published.* I said that the book was also an exposé of the cover-up of alternative treatments of cancer.

'I haven't had much respect for modern medical methods for years,' I told him. 'I think American medicine is superb in its treatment of traumas, but, with degenerative or other diseases, I feel many of the treatments are useless, even harmful. It's never seemed to help you, and I lost several good years taking the drugs the psychiatrist prescribed for

---

* My book was published in 1978 and is now out of print. However, if you want to know how I overcame cancer you can obtain a reprint of my article, 'A Personal Cancer Cure', published in *Mother Earth News*, No. 56, March/April 1979. For details please send a stamped self-addressed envelope to P.O. Box No. 2045, Fair Oaks, CA 95628.

me. When I learned about the cancer, I decided I'd rather trust myself than the prevailing cancer treatments. I was able to find doctors and others who have treated cancer without using radiation, surgery or chemotherapy. With the help of these courageous people, I overcame cancer in a few months' time.'

Richard was intensely interested in the exposé part of the book and read the manuscript over the weekend. He became indignant about the power the vested interests have in the treatment of cancer.

'I've been lecturing at health conventions recently,' I told him, 'and I met Ann Wigmore of the Hippocrates Health Institute in Boston. She told me that they have helped people with epilepsy reduce their medications by living in the institute for several months. It takes that long to adjust the medications and change the diet and lifestyle. They have a holistic programme there which reaches all levels of life. I found that I needed help physically, emotionally, mentally and spiritually to overcome cancer. I feel better than I've ever felt in my life. I'm even glad I had the cancer because the changes I've had to make have so enhanced my life. Would you consider going to Boston to try it?'

'That would take months,' Richard said. 'How do I know it would help?'

'You don't. But wouldn't it be worth a try?'

He didn't answer, so I backed off once again.

I saw Richard several weekends after that. I would drop him off at an Emotions Anonymous meeting as I went to my own Twelve–step meeting. One evening as we drove home after the meetings, he shared an incident that was amusing to him.

'I walked into the meeting and noticed that people looked at me with surprise. Most of them were quite obese. As the meeting progressed, I realized that I was in an Overeaters Anonymous meeting.' He had that bashful grin on his face.

'I left and found my own meeting which had moved across the hall.'

Richard could still be amused at life's situations and that made my heart glad.

7
We Lose Contact with Richard

About this time Richard moved to Ventura. I didn't see him again until David's wedding late in 1977. Richard was wearing the sports coat I had given him the year before. His shirt was filthy around the collar. I felt embarrassed for him. I had heard from his father that Richard had been on a trip.

During the reception I said, 'Tell me about your trip.'

Richard seemed very proud. He became animated as he talked. 'I travelled through every one of the 48 states and even got into Canada and Mexico. I bought a bus ticket for $75.00 and took a sleeping bag and travelled for months. In New York I was mugged and lost my medications, but I was able to get more. It was quite a trip.'

'I'm glad you had such a great experience,' I said. I was also relieved that I hadn't known what he was doing. I would have been so worried.

All of the family lost contact with Richard after that. My ex-husband confided in me one day. 'One can agonize about someone only so long. I just don't feel well enough to have him over any more. I don't know where Richard is now. The last cheque I mailed him was returned.'

When his father died of cancer in October of 1979, we had to trace Richard through the Social Security office. He was still living in Sacramento. We didn't locate him in time for him to attend his father's funeral. When David finally talked with Richard, he told him that each of the children would be receiving money from their father's estate.

Richard told David that he was sorry he had not seen his father before he died.

At Christmas time in 1979, Richard called David and came down for a few days. Ann and I spent Christmas with

David and his new wife, too. Driving over I braced myself to see Richard. When we met I observed him surreptitiously. He now had white scaly spots on his face and hands. A front tooth was missing.

I tried to give him a hug, but he backed away. 'What happened to your tooth?' I asked.

'I finally lost that tooth. It had been dead since that accident from the seizure years ago, and they finally had to pull it. It's so difficult to get any dental work done through Medi-Cal that I haven't been able to get a bridge.'

He was still wearing the sports coat I'd given him several years ago. It badly needed cleaning and pressing. Despite all, he still had a very boyish and immature look about him. His manner was still shy and tentative.

I gave Richard a thick, warm jacket for Christmas.

A few days after Christmas, I took Richard to a restaurant. He never refused a dinner invitation. He ate voraciously as usual, but conversation was sparse. My cancer book had finally been published. I showed him one of my flyers outlining the workshops and tapes I offered. He had no comment.

He didn't seem excited about the prospect of receiving the money, a sum of around $40,000. As soon as he had finished eating, he became restless and wanted to leave. I drove him back to David's house.

A few months after, on 11 July 1980, my first grandchild, Adam, was born. Around his first birthday, I called David, who was a house-husband at that time, and was writing a screen play.

'Can I take Adam to the park?'

'Sure, come on over. Stay as long as you like; it will give me time to write.'

When Adam and I got to the park, I followed him around as he toddled about exploring. His blue eyes sparkled, and his softly curling brown hair framed his handsome face.

An older woman sitting on a bench remarked, 'What a handsome child.'

'That's my grandson, Adam,' I crowed.

After that first outing, Adam and I experienced much joy together every week. I felt a deep bond between us that I had never experienced before. I didn't know until then that I had never bonded with anyone before that time. By this time my children were grown. I sobbed for days because the intimacy and joy I experienced with Adam had been impossible between me and my children. What a loss for all of us!

Had my not being able to bond caused Richard's problems? Could some other mother have done more for him? David and Ann weren't like Richard despite our lack of intimacy. I hoped to heal my relationships with David and Ann too, as I continued to heal myself. I had learned only recently how my own stark, emotionally abandoned and abusive childhood had contributed to my unease with my own children, and to my alcoholism and cancer.

I didn't see Richard again until November 1981 when he came to collect the cheque from his father's estate. The cheque had been at the lawyer's office for several months. Richard seemed reluctant to receive the money. I didn't understand why until later.

I might not have seen him at all if David had not had to leave Adam with me while he drove Richard to the lawyer's office. After their visit to the lawyer, Richard came in with David, walked up to me and said, 'The lawyer said that you wanted to see me. Can you tell me the reason?'

'I wanted to be sure you got your money,' I said.

'Oh,' he replied.

The meeting was awkward. As we were standing there ineptly, Adam started to cry. He was hungry and wanted to go home. David scooped him into his arms, said his good-bye, and the three of them walked out. That was the last time I saw Richard.

I was busy building a career of lecturing, counselling, teaching and writing. My heart never stopped aching for Richard, but I had learned that the only life I could live was mine. I prayed for him every day. I worked on all levels to stay healthy. I studied constantly, searching for answers to the purpose and meaning of life, especially mine and Richard's. I felt I had discovered why I had had cancer: I hadn't had an identity, I hadn't been a person, plus I hadn't been using my creativity. Other than that, I was still in the dark about life and its meaning. I would have to be patient. I knew I had lost years of spiritual guidance because drugs and alcohol block contact with the spiritual worlds. I felt deeply that Richard was lost because drugs now blocked him and had done so since he was 15 years old. I finally had to accept that I could do nothing to help him.

8
Across the Threshold

On Friday, 2 July 1982, I was writing in my journal when I was inundated with such agony of soul, with such deep and overpowering feelings of hopelessness and despair, I felt nauseous. I lay the journal aside and walked into the living room so I could see the ocean, which always calms me. The sun was shining brightly on the white caps. I saw a lone seagull flying gracefully over a sailing-boat, which was bobbing gently in the waves.

Where are these feelings coming from? What are they trying to tell me, I asked myself. The feelings came crashing in waves fiercer than the ocean that day. They had started suddenly and had no relation to my own life. These feelings continued for days.

On Tuesday afternoon, 13 July, still experiencing those feelings, I heard the phone ring. The probate officer who had handled my ex-husband's estate was on the line.

'Can you come in this afternoon? I need to talk with you about something I can't discuss on the phone.'

I couldn't imagine what she wanted. My ex-husband's estate had been settled for over a year.

'You'll have to tell me on the phone,' I responded. 'I can't come down there.'

'I received a call from Detective Gordon from the Seattle Missing Persons-Mental Investigations Unit. He said he fears Richard has drowned. It seems Richard rented a canoe on Sunday, and a couple of hours later a passer by found the canoe abandoned about a mile from the boat house. Detective Gordon has spent the last two days trying to find Richard's family. He found no personal papers, letters, addresses or phone numbers in Richard's belongings. He was able to trace him because there was a letter from our office. He called me and I told him I'd tell you. I'm so sorry. If I can help in any way, please, let me know.'

She gave me Detective Gordon's phone number and we disconnected.

My God! This was finally it! I knew he was gone. I knew he had finally had enough. I felt a tremendous stab of pain in my heart.

With a shock I realized that those feelings of despair and hopelessness I had felt for days had come from Richard!

I hugged myself closely, rocking back and forth trying to hold myself together. When I felt I could speak coherently, I picked up the phone and called Detective Gordon.

'Have you found Richard's body? Are they dragging the lake? What do you think happened?' I talked without stopping for an answer.

The detective said, 'Perhaps you can help me piece together what may have happened. We found no suicide note, but the circumstances could point to suicide. His wallet, which had $50 in cash and a bank deposit slip for $20,000, was carefully laid in the bottom of the canoe along with his shoes, a tote bag, and some books. He either drowned or wants someone to believe he did. Did he have any reason to fake a suicide?

'No,' I replied, 'and he wouldn't leave his wallet or a bank deposit behind. He could never survive without his SSI. He's never worked or been able to support himself financially.'

Detective Gordon continued, 'I searched his apartment, which had a mess of papers and letters to newspapers and magazines. His apartment is located in the meanest, cheapest section of Seattle where it isn't safe to venture out at night. His checking account has a balance of over $17,000. Why would he live in such horrible circumstances with that kind of money?'

'He inherited about $40,000 from his father last year. He's

never been able to work and has lived on SSI for many years. His inheritance isn't enough to enable him to live elaborately for very long. He probably planned to use it for special occasions and live as he had before,' I surmised.

'His apartment manager informed me that he had planned to move to Alaska. He said that Richard had no visitors or telephone and only went out during the day. At night he stayed home with the door bolted. Would he have had any reason to disappear? Were the police after him? If it's suicide, why wouldn't he leave a note?'

My head was spinning. The picture of that apartment and Richard being utterly alone with literally no one to call and no one to call him was unbearable.

'He wouldn't think to leave a note. His taking off his shoes and leaving the wallet in full view in the canoe was his way of making sure he could be traced, or maybe it was an impulse of the moment brought on by overwhelming feelings of despair. He has had such a tragic life. He has been suicidal before and has been deteriorating mentally and physically for many years. Are you searching for the body?'

'No. It is quite common not to recover a drowning victim in Lake Washington. The lake is very deep and very cold. Most times they are never recovered, or we've had instances of bodies surfacing after several years in the water. There's no way we can search for the body. I have alerted the border patrol, and they will watch the currents for a body. We may be lucky. He disappeared within two hours of renting the canoe, but there was no trace of his body near the canoe. We'll leave the investigation open for a few days. If nothing shows up, I'll have the apartment manager send you his effects. I will put his bank books in safekeeping until I close the case. You had better contact the bank and tell them what happened. I tend to think it is suicide, too.'

I heard the apartment door open. My daughter, Ann, stood in the doorway.

'I fear Richard is dead,' I said.

Her eyes opened in horror. 'What happened,' she asked.

'Let me call David, and I'll tell you as much as I know.'

I was still in shock. We drove along the ocean, through El Segundo to Westchester, where David lived. The sun was shining on the breakers. I saw an oil tanker off shore. I told Ann all I knew on the way and later repeated it to David.

David hadn't seen or heard from Richard since the New Year. We didn't know that he was in Seattle.

'We are fortunate to know what happened to him,' I said. 'I've always been afraid he'd just disappear, and we'd never know whether he was alive or dead. Detective Gordon was surprised that Richard had nothing to connect him with another human being except the lawyer. He tends to think it is suicide, and I'm sure of it. David, if they do recover his body, would you go up there and identify it? I don't think I could bear to do that.'

David said he would.

The three of us were horrified. Richard had been on his own for eleven years by this time, and each of us had gone on with our lives. Neither Ann nor David felt a connection with Richard, who had cast such a shadow over the family.

'I'll keep you informed of any developments,' I said. 'I am going home to call the priest at American Martyrs to offer mass for Richard in the morning. When they close the case, I will put an announcement in the paper and have a memorial mass said. I want to call Gerry Connell and other families who knew Richard when he was attending American Martyrs' school. After the memorial mass, I'd like the three of us to spend some time together.'

As we drove back home along the ocean, other thoughts flooded my mind. I had read a lot in the past few years about life after death, two books just the week before, and I knew from them that suicide is a horrible choice. I recalled Dr George G. Ritchie's book *Return from Tomorrow*, which tells the plight of several people who had committed suicide.

Ritchie's book recounts his experiences during several minutes when he had a near-death experience in December 1943. A figure of light had come to him and had taken him on a tour of the world of the dead. When this presence had appeared to Ritchie, he wrote that he realized with certainty that he had been in the presence of the Son of God. This presence took him through many places.

One of these places contained several pictures that were the same in nature. A young man who was dead kept following his father around saying how sorry he was, that he didn't know what it would do to his mother. His father couldn't hear him and wasn't even aware he was there.

In another scene a boy trailed a teenage girl through the corridors of the school saying, 'I'm sorry.' After several similar scenes, Ritchie asked his guide why they were so sorry? Why did they keep talking to people who couldn't hear them? Then the presence told him that they were suicides and were chained to the consequences of their acts.

My mind raced to Dr Moody's book *Life after Life*, in which he recounts the experience of many who have had near-death experiences. Concerning those who had tried to commit suicide and almost died, he writes that each one had the same experience. They knew immediately that they had done the wrong thing. One experienced being in a horrible 'limbo' and had the feeling that he would be there for a long time. I felt frantic about Richard.

As I pulled into the driveway, I wanted to make two phone calls immediately. The first was to the priest to offer mass the next morning. The other was to a clairvoyant friend who I knew could find Richard for me. I also wanted to talk with my former friends who had known Richard and accepted him. My current friends had never met Richard.

I felt some relief after I arranged for the mass the following morning. I was praying for Richard in between phone calls, asking God to help him and to have mercy on his soul. When I reached the clairvoyant friend, she said

Richard was feeling overwhelming remorse, and realized immediately after death that he was worse off than ever. She did share one ray of light, however.

'Richard chose to leave without involving anyone else, and he made sure that you would be informed by leaving his wallet in the canoe. That will ameliorate his suffering somewhat,' she said compassionately.

I started calling my old friends who had known Richard and asked them to pray. I kept my panic at bay by talking about him. My old Irish friend, Gerry Connell, comforted me by saying that Richard would not be judged so harshly because of his lifelong problems.

Detective Gordon called a couple of days later. 'I am closing the file on Richard,' he said. 'The case is not closed with the Medical Examiner's office, however, since there is no body.'

He told me also that a reporter for the Bellview newspaper, the *Journal American,* had called him when he saw the report of Richard's apparent drowning in the *Post Intelligencer* newspaper. The reporter said he had talked with Richard a few days before his death and had written about Richard in an article. Detective Gordon gave me his telephone number and address and that of the Chief Medical Examiner who was responsible for issuing a death certificate.

I immediately called the reporter, Mike Merritt, and left a message. I wanted to learn all he knew of Richard, since their meeting was so close to his death.

I then called the local newspaper and placed a notice of his death with the time of his funeral mass. After the notice appeared, we received several cards and offerings of perpetual masses for him from families we had known when Richard was a child.

The day of the funeral mass, Gerry Connell slipped beside me in the pew and held my hand. When the mass was over, I walked out to the entry of the church. Several other old friends were there and came up and comforted us.

When Richard's effects reached me, I placed his estate into probate and started the heart-wrenching task of sorting his papers. I discovered almost immediately what I thought to be the final push to his death. Richard was being audited by the IRS because of the money he had received from his father. His SSI and Medi-Cal had been cancelled as of 1 June, five and a half weeks before his death. What would he have done after his money had been spent? No wonder he lived in a slum. He didn't have the ability to go through re-qualifying for SSI after the money was gone. I hadn't realized that he would lose SSI because of receiving money that certainly couldn't support him for more than a few years.

Later, I discovered this was only one of the painful things in Richard's life at that time. His life had been a shambles on all fronts. As I continued to sort through the papers, I found several letters he was composing, one of which was to an author. In this letter I found a quote that seemed to me to symbolize his life, and I stopped immediately and composed my salute to his life as follows:

In Memoriam
Richard Alan Deverell
1946–1982
When I think of Richard, I think of courage.

A stranger to this earth, he was never comfortable here and was seldom accepted by others. Most every time he ventured out the door, he met with rejection. He never discovered why he couldn't relate. On mind-altering drugs since age 15 to control epilepsy, he was out of touch with his inner self. He felt himself to be a failure and the world would judge him so.

But I say, 'Judge not by appearances.' Who knows but God the courage Richard showed to keep on keeping on.

One of the last things Richard wrote in a letter to the author, Claudette Dowling, was: 'The only real crime is the crime of unreality and the refusal to search for a healthier, freer, and more independent outlook about society in general and personal motivation in particular.'

Richard never gave up the search. He is now taking a 'coffee break' to rest and regroup his energy. He'll be back another time to continue his work here on planet earth.

I salute you, Richard, for your courage. I send you love to welcome you to your new place.

Your mother this time around.

Also in his belongings was a notebook with a list of his resentments, which was part of a fourth step he had taken in an alcoholic recovery programme. I was surprised to learn that he had been an alcoholic. One resentment caught my eye. A therapist in his therapy group had said to Richard, 'One day you'll commit suicide and that'll be the end of you.' What an insensitive thing to say! What kind of a therapist was that? I put the notebook down. I couldn't bear to know any more. In fact, I quickly burned all of his papers. I couldn't bear prying into his life like that.

I also disposed of his clothes, which were not good enough to take to the Goodwill. One of the items I threw out was a green sweater which I had knit 20 years before when he was 16 years old. Is it possible he had kept that for sentimental reasons? After disposing of his things, I felt a bit of a completion. I felt it was time to move on, to let go of the past. I would continue to pray daily for Richard. But this was not the end of the story.

9
One Search Ends, Another Begins

When I contacted the office of the Medical Examiner for the death certificate, he refused to issue one. Instead, he requested that I put together a personality profile and background on Richard to show that Richard could not live without money and medical care. His reasoning was that Richard could have chosen to disappear for reasons unknown.

'Oh, no!' I thought to myself. 'Can't I ever be free of this? How much longer can this go on?' The bank wouldn't release Richard's money without a death certificate, and the State of California had already filed a request to the lawyer to be apprised of Richard's estate as they might claim all of it to repay the state for medical services to Richard over the years. I had no choice but to comply.

That request from the coroner began a search that lasted for three months which pieced together a picture of Richard's life since he had been on disability, particularly during the last six months before his death. The picture was bleak indeed. I had to gather evidence from the California State Welfare Department, from the Social Security Department, from former doctors, from Kaiser Permanente, his medical provider in Los Angeles, from the Department of Health Services in Sacramento, and others.

I obtained a report from Dr Alexander Sweel, the psychiatrist who had examined Richard at the request of the Department of Public Social Services to determine eligibility for disability. In the letter he stated that he had seen Richard about a hundred times. He said that Richard was suffering from epilepsy and chronic severe schizophrenia. He explained that there was evidence of mental and intellectual deterioration from a long-standing seizure disorder and mental illness. He said that Richard's prognosis was very poor and that there was no possibility of a cure for his problems. I had just returned from lunch with a friend when this letter arrived. I was shocked to see in black and white how desperate Richard's condition had been. I had never completely given up hope that he could be healed.

The news reporter from Washington sent me a copy of the article he had written that mentioned Richard. The reporter had been investigating Companions, a defunct dating service, and had met Richard three days before his death. Richard was peering into the window of their former office, now empty of all furniture, although the phones still had not yet been disconnected and were ringing constantly. The reporter rightly surmised that Richard had been a client and queried him. Richard said he had been at the office the week before because he had paid them $695 with the promise that they would introduce him to a woman within 15 days. The contract Richard signed promised him at least 20 introductions over a period of a year. Richard hadn't received any introductions and had come to make enquiries.

Richard confided to the reporter, 'They made me feel like a culprit. I feel at least partly to blame because I failed to examine the service's promises closely enough.'

In his letter to me the reporter confessed that he was puzzled that Richard seemed not much concerned about the loss of the money. He added that Richard seemed like a lonely person. The reporter called the police when he saw the announcement of Richard's apparent drowning. Here was another unsuccessful attempt to make a connection with another human being which had cost him $695.

I received a letter from Dr Robert Wellauer at Kaiser Permanente who stated that Richard would never be able to function because of his extreme difficulty relating to others and conversing. The doctor said he had last seen Richard on

9 June 1978, because of a head injury and headaches. God only knows what caused the head injury.

The Department of Health and Human Services (SSI) reported that Richard had been receiving disability until 1 June 1982, when his cheques were terminated because of his receiving money from his father's estate. The letter stated that Richard had been involved in a vocational rehabilitation programme, but that he had only worked during the period of May 1979 through July 1979. So, the department had tried to make Richard self-supporting with no success. This was new information.

I obtained records from the Department of Health Services in Sacramento that revealed the last two times Richard had sought medical help, once in November and once in December 1981.

After I had gathered the evidence to show that Richard was certainly dead and had not deliberately disappeared, I wrote a three-page, single-spaced, typewritten letter to the Chief Medical Examiner requesting a death certificate. When I read the completed letter, I wondered what other traumas Richard had experienced. On receipt of the letter, the coroner's office immediately notified the Bureau of Vital Statistics to issue a death certificate for Richard.

With the death certificate the lawyer finalized Richard's estate. For some miraculous reason the State of California declined to claim any portion of Richard's money. The money came to me.

I vowed to use the money to help others like Richard. To do that I felt I first had to find an understanding for his life. I didn't know how or where, but I would! I couldn't bear to believe that Richard's life had been meaningless.

I stormed heaven for answers. I knew they were out there somewhere. One morning during meditation, I yelled at the spiritual world: 'What do you want from me?'

In a soft voice the answer came, 'Maybe, you could be in on the development of children.'

I sat there stunned. Me? Be in on the development of children? Me? Who had felt such a failure as a mother? What could this mean?

I called my friend, Anna. 'Guess what I got in meditation this morning? That maybe I could help in the development of children!'

'Oh,' she exclaimed, 'That sounds like the training offered by Rudolf Steiner College in Sacramento. I received a brochure from them recently. Shall we drive up to investigate? I'm looking for a new direction myself.'

Within days we were on our way to Sacramento. I felt I was home the moment I stepped on campus. I felt strongly that the answers I sought, had been seeking for years, would be found here at last.

Part II

HEALING

10
Finding a New Beginning

Rudolf Steiner College is located in Fair Oaks, California, about 16 miles north-east of downtown Sacramento. When we arrived at the campus that sunny Sunday afternoon in April 1983, Anna and I walked onto a driveway made of embedded cement blocks. Grass was growing through the block openings alongside a house that had been converted to the dining hall and classroom.

As we passed the house and turned right, we stepped onto a curving path of wooden slats which led to a large, unusually shaped building of a weathered grey colour. Huge trees built a breathtaking canopy over several picnic tables scattered around the grounds. Flower beds were filled with luxuriant plants, the healthiest I had ever seen. The building had two entrances, one at either end, each angling out from the edifice. The glass in the doors had interesting shapes instead of the usual rectangles.

Then I was drawn to a piece of land that stretched as far as the eye could see. At the entry to this land was a flower garden bursting with every imaginable colour and texture. The land was not cultivated beyond the garden and was dotted with trees. A fence running along one side separated a pasture next door which held playful horses.

'Anna, isn't that a peaceful scene? We would have to drive many miles in Los Angeles to see something like this.'

We paused there for a few moments before exploring the rest of the grounds. We found six more small structures. Throughout the grounds the curving, wooden path passed by mounds of flower beds. A weathered brick fence stood between the front house and the smaller buildings. In the front of the administration house a gnarled, old, strong oak tree spread its huge expanse over mounds of wild flowers bordering the parking lot.

'Anna, does the place exhilarate you as much as it does me?'

'It is unique and makes me want to explore their courses,' she replied.

We left the college and went to a Good Earth restaurant near the motel for dinner. Large green plants served as dividers between tables. The pace was slow and relaxed—a good antidote for my rising excitement. After we ordered, I said:

'I know I'm going to attend that college. I feel I'm home at last.'

Anna's blue eyes twinkled in reply. 'You don't have your interview until tomorrow. How can you be so sure?'

I'm not sure very often in this life, but when I'm sure, I'm sure. How do you feel? Do you think they have what you want?'

'I'll wait and see,' she said.

The following morning I kept my appointment with the registrar, a bustling, cheery woman, who led me into her office, which she shared with another staff person.

'We offer a two-year training course to prepare Waldorf teachers.* The first year is the Foundation Year, followed by a year of Teacher Training. We also have an Arts Program for those who would like a year of art. Which one interests you?'

'I want to take the two-year training, then I'll see about the Arts Program,' I replied.

I filled out an application, and I bought the five basic

---

*Waldorf education—Waldorf schools are non-demoninational and independent, offering kindergarten through twelfth grade. The curriculum is based on an understanding of the developing human being, seen through the application of the spiritual science of Anthroposophy. Over 900 Waldorf schools are spread throughout the world.

books by Rudolf Steiner* which form the foundation for the course of study at the college.

She handed me a sheet. 'Here is a schedule of classes you will be taking in the fall.'

I glanced at the titles. I had never heard of these subjects before. Here was a course of instruction in which the inner human being was regarded with essential importance! My exhilaration mounted with each course title: Karma and Reincarnation, Christology, Evolution of Consciousness, Knowledge of Higher Worlds—to name a few. Liberally spread throughout these courses were the arts: eurythmy,† painting, sculpture, drawing, choir, woodworking, drama, speech and more.

'I can't believe it,' I exclaimed. 'I've finally found a place that is teaching what I want to know. I've stopped attending the state colleges because what they taught there seemed mostly irrelevant to my life.'

'I don't think you'll have that problem here,' the registrar laughed.

Materials in hand, we climbed in the car for the return trip to Los Angeles.

'Do you think you'll decide to join me at the college,' I asked Anna.

'No, it isn't exactly what I'm looking for. I'm happy for you, though.'

---

* Rudolf Steiner, Ph.D. (1861–1925) is a respected and well published scientific, literary and philosophical scholar. He developed his philosophical principles into an approach to methodical research of psychological and spiritual phenomena. His multi-faceted genius has led to innovative and holistic approaches in medicine, science, education (Waldorf schools), special education, philosophy, religion, economics, agriculture, architecture, drama, the new art of eurythmy and other fields. His published works in these fields are contained in more than 300 volumes. In 1924 he founded the General Anthroposophical Society, which today has branches throughout the world.

† Eurythmy is speech made visible through movements of the body expressing the gestures of the sounds.

'I'm so grateful that you told me about the college and could come up here with me. I've felt so abandoned most of my life. Now I can look back and see that God has been holding me in the palm of his hand the whole time.'

My voice broke and I stopped talking for a moment.

'A clairvoyant friend told me over three years ago that there would be a death in my family which would change the direction of my life. She said I would turn my back on everything I had worked so hard for to take up something totally different. How right she was! My vow to help others like Richard has led me here. His money pays my way. Do you suppose it's possible some good will come out of all this pain?'

Anna patted my arm. 'I'm sure of it,' she said.

After I dropped Anna at her apartment in San Pedro, my excitement was abated somewhat at the thought of leaving my children, and especially my grandson, Adam. He wasn't even three years old yet. I started to cry at the thought of parting from him. The first joyful relationship in my life and I had to leave! My inner child came out to play only when I was with Adam. However, I knew this was my first step in keeping my promise to Richard. I would visit my children and Adam as often as possible.

Before I left my children, I hoped to help them find healing, too. I still blamed myself for our painful relationships, even after 14 years in a recovery programme, and after working diligently to heal myself and the family. I invited them one evening and told them of my intention to move to Sacramento. I didn't tell them the vow I had made to use Richard's money to help others like him. I didn't think they'd understand, especially since I didn't know yet how I would be able to be such a helper.

I told them about ACA—Adult Children of Alcoholics—a fairly new Twelve-step programme designed for adults who were affected by their parents' alcoholism. I gave them literature about the programme. I even offered to pay for them to attend a therapy group facilitated by an ACA-trained therapist. Both refused the offer.

Within weeks I was ready to move. The day finally came when the moving van picked up my furniture. I loaded my new Honda Civic hatchback with my plants and portable TV and headed north on Highway 99.

By school's opening in the fall, I would be 60 years old, and I could start receiving social security cheques from my husband's contributions. I felt fortunate indeed, despite my feeling lonely for my grandson, Adam, and my children.

11
Reading to Richard

After I settled into my apartment, I went exploring. I visited the Sacramento Waldorf School, which was a block away from the college. The school was located near the American River, a group of buildings with many trees and huge fields for outdoor activities.

I found a tree on the bank overlooking the rapids and quickly claimed it for my 'thinking' spot. I sat there and read from the five basic books so I would be as ready as possible for the fall classes. Though I was eager for school to begin, not a day passed that I didn't pray for Richard and for the healing of the family relationships.

I called Ann weekly, and she came for a three-day visit for her twentieth birthday. I had already given a workshop and was teaching classes at the Creative Awareness Center on holistic health.

Classes finally began the week after Labor Day. The 50 students made my class fairly large. I noticed two other women in my age group. Several countries were represented, and I looked forward to meeting such interesting-looking people.

One day, a few weeks after school started, I was having lunch with a classmate when I confided to her about Richard. Her brown eyes filled with compassion. Then she had a thought and her eyes lit up.

'Did you know that Rudolf Steiner says that it helps the dead to read to them?'

'No!' I exclaimed. 'How can I find out about that?'

'You can call Richard Lewis, a Christian Community priest. He can give you the details.'

She gave me his number.

'Thank you so much for telling me this,' I said as I gave her a hug and rushed for the pay telephone in the dining hall.

I had attended a service once at the Christian Community Church when I'd first moved to Sacramento. As I dialled the number, my mind raced. I felt certain such reading would help Richard.

Richard Lewis himself answered the phone. I told him what I was after. He said, indeed, it helped to read to the dead. The priest told me several places in Steiner's books where he encourages people to read to those who have passed over.

'Reading to the dead is very beneficial to them. They are starving for spiritual food while going through the first experiences after death.* Reading to them provides great nourishment,' Reverend Lewis explained.

'What do you suggest I read?' I asked.

'Any spiritually inspired works would be fine: the Bible, especially the John Gospel (Chapters 13 through 17), poetry, meditative verses, spiritual songs. Of course, any of Rudolf Steiner's works are excellent. Did your son have a special interest?' he asked.

'Music,' I answered.

'Steiner gave a series of lectures on music. I'm sure the College has a copy in its library. That would be a good place to start. Everything you're reading for your classes would be great also. The five basic books are the foundation for the rest of his work.'

'How does one go about it?' I queried further. He gave me some instructions† and then rang off with the promise that he would send me some verses that Steiner had written

---

* Kamaloca is the period one spends after death reviewing the past life in reverse. The time spent there is roughly one third of a person's life.
† See Appendix I, 'One Way to Read to the Dead'

especially for the dead. I could use these to call Richard to me before I began reading. I felt elated.

After classes I went into the library and checked out the book about music.* I was eager to get home and prepare a special place where I would do the reading. I placed a picture of Richard on a table with a candle. I felt happy doing it.

The verses arrived the following afternoon. The next morning I reviewed the instructions the priest had given me. He had explained that I didn't need to read aloud. The dead don't hear with ears; it is the thoughts that reach them. Therefore, it is very important to think as deeply and as clearly as possible about what one is reading. Since I found Steiner's work extremely difficult to penetrate, I knew I would be reading carefully anyway to understand the material.

I imagined Richard, and other family members and friends who had died, standing before me and I called each one by name. Striving to be as totally involved as possible with the material, I filled myself with loving thoughts for each one of them.

'Dear Christ, please protect me while reading to the dead,' I asked. Reverend Lewis said this was necessary because the dead have different vibrations which can upset our metabolism. I lit the candle and began the verses.

> Spirit of his soul, effective guardian
> May your wings convey my soul's petitioning love
> To this human in the spheres
> Entrusted to your care
> So that, united with your power,
> My love may radiate helpfully
> To the soul it seeks in love.

---

*Rudolf Steiner, *The Inner Nature of Music and the Experience of Tone*, Anthroposophic Press, NY.

I look to you in the spirit world
In which you are.
May my love mitigate your heat,
May my love mitigate your cold,
May it come through to you and help you
To find the way
From the spirit's darkness
To the spirit's light.

What a beautiful verse. My heart filled with compassion as I read the stanzas, especially the last one. I told Richard that I was sorry that I hadn't been able to help him more while he was on earth, but that I felt finally something would help him. Then I started reading the first lecture of *The Inner Nature of Music*.

Something on the third page caught my attention: 'When the musician composes, he cannot imitate anything. He must draw the motifs of musical creation out of his soul.'*

I paused as I recalled a conversation Richard and I had had once. I don't remember what we were discussing, but I had finished my argument by saying that if Richard had composed, maybe he could have found his soul. 'I found my soul when I found music,' Richard had responded.

I felt my understanding of Richard grow as I was reading. I began to have glimpses into his soul that were hidden from me by his difficult personality while on earth.

Further on, I read: 'Physical music is but a reflection of the spiritual reality. A tone lies at the foundation of everything in the physical world.'†

I could imagine that this pleased Richard immeasurably. He had always searched for the source of things.

In this first lecture I learned that, when we sleep, we are awake in the spiritual worlds but aren't conscious of this

---

* Ibid., p. 3.
† Ibid. pp. 5, 6.

unless we are clairvoyant. When a human being sleeps during the night 'the soul feasts and lives in flowing tone ... which is the soul's true home.'*

Each sentence was more wondrous than the former one. The lecture ended with, 'The archetype of music is in the spiritual, whereas the archetypes for the other arts lie in the physical world itself. When the human being hears music, he has a sense of well-being because these tones harmonize with what he has experienced in the world of his spiritual home.'†

This first reading was profound. It explained why Richard was able to lose himself in music and not care for the world around him. I believe his tragedy was that, once he had to take drugs for epilepsy, his ability to tune into his soul was impossible—which explained why he'd never composed after his first seizure. I sobbed for his loss.

The following day, as I read, I learned that man experiences music with his whole being: 'An orchestra is an image of man.' Then came the panorama of how the evolution of music and the evolution of humanity go hand in hand. Indeed, 'The facts of human evolution are expressed in musical development more clearly than anywhere else.'‡

When I finished reading this book to Richard, I felt the grandeur of being human and great reverence and awe for the higher spiritual beings involved in our evolution. I liked to think that these thoughts were taking the place of Richard's dark thoughts of despair.

I read at least one lecture every day, and sometimes two or three. In class we had just begun studying *Knowledge of Higher Worlds and Its Attainment*.§ Each evening I included

---

* Ibid. p. 5.
† Ibid. p. 9
‡ Ibid. p. 70.
§ Rudolf Steiner, *Knowledge of Higher Worlds and Its Attainment*, Anthroposophic Press, NY. Also available as *How to Know Higher Worlds*, Anthroposophic Press.

Richard when I worked on my assignments. This book presents much knowledge of the spiritual worlds. It is also a handbook showing how to develop faculties of spiritual perception through exercises and soul attitudes. As I read those first few sentences, I wondered how much of the spiritual worlds Richard could see. I knew that suicides are isolated after death. At least, with the reading, he could learn about them.

Once again, as I continued reading, I saw more deeply into Richard. For example, the fundamental attitude of soul needed to begin training to reach the higher worlds is called the 'path of veneration, of devotion to truth and knowledge.'*

As I read, I realized Richard's passion in searching for truth and knowledge over many years. How unconscious I had been of Richard's essence while it was covered over with his illness and with my anxiety about him. I hoped Richard realized now that he had had that quality of devotion to truth.

Some days I read for hours at a time. I learned as I continued reading that before one can reach the spiritual worlds it is necessary to confront the evil in oneself and to transform it. This transformation gradually enables one to see more of one's life's purpose, and one's understanding of life grows. 'In the past he [the spiritual pupil] knew not why he laboured and suffered, but now he knows. He knows that his labour and suffering are given and endured for the sake of a great, spiritual, cosmic whole.'†

I wondered what purpose Richard's great suffering had fulfilled in the cosmic whole. Which part of his suffering had been from past deeds? Or had he taken on a cosmic assignment? How little I knew of my son, really.

After Christmas we began a study of *The Philosophy of*

---

* Ibid., p. 5.
† Ibid. p. 14.

*Freedom.** This book clearly defines what true freedom and true morality are. Step by step it shows that freedom only comes to us through the development of our morality. I learned that my act is only free and appropriate when I act out of love for the deed.

One of the most exciting things I had learned so far about freedom explained many enigmas to me. We humans are the only beings in the cosmos who have been given free will, the ability to make choices. To make choices we had to have something to choose from. Hence, good or evil, love or hate, faith or doubt. I began to feel what an awesome responsibility I have as a human to be given the chance for freedom, and how unfree I had been when addicted to alcohol, tobacco, coffee and wanting the approval of others at any cost—not to mention having to overcome all of the untruths I had learned from parents, religion and education. On the other hand, freedom is frightening too. It provides no authority to guide me—or to blame for my troubles!

I could feel that this book greatly affected Richard. Richard and I had discussed morality more than once. He vehemently believed that morality couldn't be legislated. He knew that morality could only come from the individual. Richard and I could have discussed this book for days. I was greatly cheered by the feeling that he was delighted with this knowledge which confirmed his own thinking.

During those first months of reading, I had no intimation of Richard's response, if any, to the content of my reading. I knew, however, that the love and attention directed to him daily must be healing him, as it was healing me. I never really had any expectation of hearing from him.

Meanwhile, I joined the local branch of the Anthro-

---

*Rudolf Steiner, *The Philosophy of Freedom*, Anthroposophic Press, NY. Also available as *Intuitive Thinking as a Spiritual Path*, Anthroposophic Press.

posophical Society (founded by Rudolf Steiner in 1924 with branches throughout the world) and attended their meetings on Wednesday evenings. I had finally found others who were as eager to know about the spiritual worlds as I.

12
Richard Responds

Reading to Richard became a daily ritual in my life. I never missed a day unless I was on vacation, when I drove to Los Angeles every school break to see my children and Adam.

Experiencing much bliss with the studies and arts at the College, I wanted to share this with Richard, too. I invited him to all presentations given at the College and to the Sacramento Symphony with me on Sunday afternoons.

Driving down the midtown streets of Sacramento to the Symphony, I had an eerie feeling about Richard having lived in Sacramento until shortly before his death. I wondered if I ever passed a house where he had once lived. Had he ever attended the Symphony? Had he attended sessions of the legislature at the Capitol? How strange that we had both moved to Sacramento. Rudolf Steiner College was here when Richard lived here, but I'm sure he never found it.

Along with reading to Richard and other family members and friends, I wrote in my journal every day and communicated with those who had died through prayer and by sending them love. In April 1984 in my Journal, I wrote, 'Oh, Christ, envelop Richard in your love, in your light, so he may love and find himself.' I felt very close to Richard at such times, though I wasn't conscious of any message from him.

In May 1984, after I had been reading to Richard for six months, and just as I was waking, he came to me. He was holding something in his hand. His face expressed happiness with a touch of surprise. 'I have finally found something that's helping me,' he told me, not in words, but in a thought. He was holding this knowledge in his hand to show me that he had received it. This was not a common dream; though he was standing before me, it was more of a sensing, not a seeing, and I knew that he was in the spiritual worlds, not in my bedroom.

As I lay there becoming more conscious, I thought about it. I began to feel elated. I had learned that the best time for the dead to approach us is when we are waking, and the best time for us to approach them is when we are falling asleep (see Appendix II). I had practised asking Richard questions before falling asleep, but this was my first conscious contact with him. I lay there wrapped in warm wonder. So, it appeared to be true that reading to the dead can alter their circumstances in the spiritual worlds! What a wonderful knowledge to have! I wanted to share it with the world.

I looked out the window and saw some white clouds drifting by. Overcome with gratitude, I started to cry. This day happened to be a Sunday. I had the luxury of lying there basking in Richard's communication. If I never heard from him again, this was worth reading to him forever.

After breakfast the phone rang. My son David was on the line. 'Happy Mother's Day,' he said. I hadn't realized until then that it was Mother's Day. My heart leaped with joy. I wondered if Richard had known it was Mother's Day. I had always felt I'd failed him as a mother. Was he trying to tell me differently? Whatever, the important thing was that my reading was helping and he was able to let me know. I had no idea if or when I'd hear from him again.

At the College we were studying *Theosophy*.* As I read to Richard, I was thrilled to learn about man as a being comprised of body, soul and spirit, with each part subject to different laws. The body lives in the physical world and is subject to the laws of heredity and nature, and so the body is mortal. The spirit is the part of us that reincarnates and is subject to the laws of reincarnation and is immortal. The soul

---

* Rudolf Steiner, *Theosophy*, Anthroposophic Press, NY (1994).

is where we experience our inner life and feelings and is subject to the laws of destiny (karma). The soul is the connecting link between the mortal and the immortal, the body and spirit. As I kept reading I started to become aware of Richard as an immortal spirit, and that he had had other lives before being my son. 'Through its actions, each human spirit has truly prepared its own destiny. It finds itself linked in each new lifetime to what it did in the previous one.'*

I had learned also that each person chooses his or her parents. Richard had chosen me. Why me? Why had we been together? Once again I asked myself, 'What had caused Richard such suffering?' How presumptuous I had been to think I had been the sole cause of his pain.

This book cleared up many questions about mortality and immortality for me. I felt I needed this knowledge to make sense out of my life and Richard's.

After theosophy we studied evolution. I read Richard the scientific details of the whole process of human and cosmic evolution, from the beginning to the next phase of earth's evolution. With growing wonder I learned that man is created in the image of God, that the reason for evolution was for humans to become as gods and become co-creators with Him. Then we, in turn, would start another evolution and bring other beings forward.

How wonderful to think in such terms; how tiresome it had been to think of my own narrow life. With a start I realized that Richard was always searching for the universal instead of the personal. Had he been ahead of the rest of us? Is that one reason we couldn't relate?

I longed to know how Richard responded to this reading. He had such a logical mind before the illness and drugs. He had read the Bible twice searching for meaning. Here at last his questions were answered in depth and comprehensively. I was sure he was grateful for this panorama.

---

* Ibid., p. 87.

My first year at the College ended. I went to Los Angeles to visit my children and Adam, who was almost four. I applied many things I had learned about the development of children to Adam. When we rode in the car, we would sing funny songs together. We painted pictures with water colours and played finger games. I started reading him fairy-tales and told him about his Guardian Angel. We had wonderful times together as always. I was finally experiencing how to be a parent.

However, the summer with Adam ended painfully. Conflict in my son's marriage splashed over onto me and Adam, and caused a rift between us. I was devastated. Thanks to practising a spiritual exercise called 'Positivity,' I chose to find something positive in the experience instead of giving into despair, resentment and blame. I wrote reams in my journal and prayed daily to have compassion and understanding. The positive I found in the experience was that I had more freedom. I had to become less dependent on Adam and find joy other ways. I prayed to be able to love all children as I loved Adam. Then I gave the relationship to Christ. The hard work paid off! By the following summer, my son asked if Adam could come visit me. He did, and we became closer than ever.

Meanwhile, I carried on with my reading and chose what I thought Richard would like most. Because of his interest in the Bible, I decided to read everything I could find that Steiner had said about the Christ. So far, what I had read to Richard had been mostly about God the Father, and not specifically about the Christ. I learned that Steiner had given many lecture cycles on Christology.

In *Christianity as Mystical Fact*,* Steiner tells that the coming of Christ had been prepared for over aeons in the Mystery centres of ancient times, where a chosen few were initiated into the spiritual worlds. Now, because of Christ's

---

* Rudolf Steiner, *Christianity as Mystical Fact*, Anthroposophic Press, NY.

death and resurrection, initiation* was for everyone who
wants to receive it and works for it. Here I learn that
initiation is a goal of life and had been happening for ages,
and I'd never heard about it in my search through the different religions. I felt reasonably sure that Richard hadn't
known about initiation either.

Steiner's lecture cycle *The Gospel of St John*† swept me up
into the realm of the Cosmic Christ. Before this, my only
reference to Christ's cosmic being was in the prologue of the
Gospel of St John in the New Testament. These powerful
words had always moved me deeply when I had attended
Catholic mass. How did Richard receive this? Could he
understand it much better than I because he didn't have a
body to dilute his reception? Was he as overjoyed as I?

In the lecture cycle *The Gospel of St Luke*,‡ Steiner paints a
picture of Christ's love and compassion. Reading these
lectures filled me with the warmth of Christ's love, which I
sent on to Richard. Could he feel it?

Next in the series, *The Gospel of St Matthew*,§ Steiner dis-
plays the many mysteries of human history and human
evolution in mighty pictures, beginning with the period
right after Noah's flood, which caused the destruction of
Atlantis, and began our post-Atlantean civilization. In this
book Steiner explains why each Gospel is so different from
the others: each one was written by an initiate who had
experienced a different initiation. They wrote from the
viewpoint of their individual initiation about Christ Jesus'
life as the model and fulfillment of all initiations. Through
Christ, initiation is available for all of us.

---

* Initiation is a process through which a teacher guides a pupil and gives
the pupil the power of looking into the spiritual worlds. There are many
kinds of initiation and many stages within each kind.
†Rudolf Steiner, *The Gospel of St John*, Anthroposophic Press, NY.
‡Rudolf Steiner, *The Gospel of St Luke*, Rudolf Steiner Press, London.
§ Rudolf Steiner, *The Gospel of St Matthew*, Rudolf Steiner Press, London.

Could Richard have been preparing for or going through an initiation? I had to let go of the ideas I had had about Richard and to admit that I knew nothing about him as a spiritual entity. Would I ever hear from him again?

Steiner's commentary in *The Gospel of St Mark*,* portrays how utterly Christ was misunderstood by all concerned. The Hebrew people didn't realize that Christ was the Messiah they had been preparing for. The Apostles didn't understand the tragic events, so they were unable to support Him. Christ had to go through the experience utterly alone, abandoned, and treated like a criminal. That's what Christ was experiencing when He said, 'My God, my God, why hast thou forsaken me?'† Here I could not hold back the tears. Richard had experienced such loneliness in his life, especially at the time of his own death. If this had been the only lifetime Richard had to live, it would have been devastating.

Of especial interest were two books that give knowledge not found in the Bible. In *The Fifth Gospel*‡ I read in depth about the life and experience of Jesus from the age of 12 to the age of 30, and the life of Christ from his arrival at the baptism in the Jordan until His crucifixion. At the crucifixion I read that, when Jesus Christ's body died on the cross, cosmic love poured into the souls of human beings and into the earth's forces.

Steiner obtained this information from the Akashic record, where every happening of humanity is stored in the spiritual world. A person who has developed the capacity can see this record if he or she can develop the spiritual organs necessary.

---

* Rudolf Steiner, *The Gospel of St Mark*, Anthroposophic Press, NY.
† *The Holy Bible*, Confraternity Edition, Catholic Book Publishing Co., NY., 1957.
‡ Rudolf Steiner, *The Fifth Gospel*, Rudolf Steiner Press, London.

In *From Jesus to Christ** I read about the difference between the human Jesus and the Cosmic Christ. Jesus had been an initiate in former lives and highly evolved. After generations of preparation by the Jewish people, Jesus had a suitable body for Christ to enter. I read with increasing wonder the depth and breadth of Christ's place in the evolution of our earth. Christ gives meaning to the whole of the evolution of earth and man.

Startling to me was the knowledge that Christ surrounds the earth and has done so since His death on the cross. To find Him and to see Him again depends on our developing the eyes of the spirit through doing spiritual exercises. Christ is here now! How I wish I could see Him. I was determined to do these exercises daily.

Both of these books contain vast amounts of knowledge in addition to the above. While reading the books to Richard, I felt my consciousness and imagined Richard's consciousness expanding joyfully to receive this precious, previously unavailable knowledge. And so the summer ended.

---

* Rudolf Steiner, *From Jesus to Christ*, Rudolf Steiner Press, London.

13
A Long Communication with Richard

When school started again in September 1984, I learned quickly that this year would be much more strenuous than the previous one. Teacher training was hard work.

One day early in the school year, more exhausted than usual, I came home from classes. I thought that I might have more rest in the mornings if I switched my reading to Richard to the evenings. Before the thought ended, I felt inundated with Richard's presence. He seemed greatly agitated and let me know he wanted to tell me something. These feelings completely took over my feeling life like the time before his death when his feelings of despair engulfed me.

I lit the candle, grabbed my daily journal so as not to lose any fleeting impressions I might receive, and concentrated on clearing my mind and listening. Not in words but in deeply troubled feelings he conveyed to me that he didn't want me to change my reading time. He was fearful I would be too tired by night-time and would skip the readings. He still needed them greatly. I assured him I would do as he wished, and he calmed down.

We had a good connection that day, and I told him how I admired his courage when he was alive. Then I reread the Memoriam to him that I had written shortly after his death. Sections spoke deeply to him:

> When I think of Richard, I think of courage . . . He felt himself to be a failure and the world would judge him so.
>
> But I say, 'Judge not by appearances.' Who knows but God the courage Richard showed to keep on keeping on . . .
>
> I salute you, Richard, for your courage. I send you love to welcome you to your new place.

Richard was greatly moved. He 'told' me, 'I didn't know you thought I had courage. I thought you saw me only as a disappointment and a failure.'

Then I received the crystal clear impression that he had made great progress in the past ten months that I had been reading to him. He gave me the feeling that he had taken responsibility for his life and for his death. He had stopped blaming others. This was thrilling news to me. I knew from my own experience that the first step on the spiritual path is to stop blaming others. Richard had taken this step! He had heard approximately 300 lectures or chapters by this time— more than 30 books.

Richard was also concerned about the family and wanted to help them. He wanted me to write David a loving letter. 'David is in a bad place right now. Ann needs help too. Keep sending them love every day as you do me.' He said he had not been able to reach his father. Richard further told me, 'I have tried to reach David and Ann, but they don't hear me. I am so glad that I can help them through you.'

My joy overflowed. In less than a year of reading Richard was able to feel love and concern for his family, which he had not been able to do while alive. I sat there trying to absorb this. This experience of Richard's being able to show he cared was so new to me.

As the experience ended, I checked the calendar and realized that it was Richard's birthday; he would have been 38 had he lived.

I wished that I was able to converse with him at any time. I didn't think I could, so I didn't even try, although I've communicated telepathically with a friend and have often picked up others' thoughts before they spoke them. I also have had knowledge of events before they happened. At this time, however, I had no idea of the new relationship my son and I were beginning, or where it would lead. This was unchartered territory for me. Furthermore, the demanding teacher training at the college took all of my energy.

Reading to him was the only way I could help at this time.

I discovered later two books written by people who were able to communicate often with a dead one over a period of years. In *Bridge Over the River,** Sigwart, a young soldier who died in World War I, was able to communicate with his sister for many years. He told her that their being able to communicate directly and often was rare, because most humans weren't developed enough. However, he said in future humans will be able to communicate as he and his sister. Until then, he stated that communication between the two worlds would come in dreams. I was grateful that I was sensitive enough to receive the dream communications.

Sigwart's sister's first awareness of Sigwart was a feeling of inner unrest, which eventually led to a strong feeling that Sigwart expected something from her. After several days of quiet solitude she realized that Sigwart wanted her to write down communications from him. She agreed to do so.

Sigwart told his family many things about the spiritual worlds, and gave them many helpful suggestions to lead a more spiritual life. Indeed, he told them, 'I, Sigwart, died for you also in order to show you the path to the spirit.'†

I identified with the feelings of unrest that Sigwart's sister felt when Sigwart wanted to communicate with her. That's how I experienced Richard's presence several times. I was glad that I was sensitive enough to feel his impulses when he was agitated.

In the other book, *Testimony of Light,*‡ Frances Banks, a nun and educator who died in November 1965, sends messages to a close co-worker, Helen Greaves. They had worked intimately together both psychically, spiritually and meditatively before Frances's death. Frances had a

---

* Wetzl, Joseph, translator, *The Bridge Over the River*, Anthroposophic Press, NY.
† Ibid., p. 32.
‡ Helen Greaves, *Testimony of Light*, Neville Spearman, Essex.

burning desire to let people on earth know about the life after death. Helen was clairaudient and Frances could reach her telepathically. They communicated for two years after Frances's death.

This last communication with Richard encouraged me to continue reading.

During classes I was learning about the difference between my blood-tie family and my spiritual family. Christ came to teach us that everyone is our brother or sister regardless of blood, race, creed or religion. I felt many people at the college and in the Anthroposophical Society were my spiritual family. That explained to me why I felt at home the moment I reached the campus.

I began the practice of trying to determine my connection to others. Rudolf Steiner gives exercises in his *Karmic Relationships*, Vol. II, p. 113,* to help discover these relationships (see Appendix III).

Having finished the books on Christology, I decided to read to Richard about life after death.† I thought this would help him recognize what he might be seeing in the spiritual worlds unless he was still in isolation due to the suicide.

I learned that immortality means to be able to be as conscious in the spiritual worlds after death as I am in the physical world during life. My degree of consciousness after death depends entirely on the consciousness of spiritual reality I develop while on earth. If my only focus in earth life is about the sense world with no thought of the spiritual worlds, then my consciousness is dimmed in the spiritual worlds and 'there is no greater fear after death than this darkening of consciousness.'‡

---

* Rudolf Steiner, *Karmic Relationships*, Vol. II, Rudolf Steiner Press, London.

† Rudolf Steiner, *Life Between Death and Rebirth*, Anthroposophic Press, NY.

‡ Ibid., p. 2.

No wonder Richard was so frantic at the thought that I might stop reading to him! He needed more light for his consciousness!

I learned that the dead are with us much of the time, and we can become conscious of them. I wished I could be conscious of Richard whenever I wanted to be. I was beginning to realize that he was conscious of me all the time.

Many of the dead experience a much broader view of life than the living. We need their expanded vision to help us make the right choices for the future. In fact, many of our inspirations come from the dead!

We can, in turn, be of great help to the dead. Reading to the dead gives nourishment to their souls like food gives nourishment to our bodies. I felt good doing this. I could picture Richard hungrily taking in every word. I felt I was finally able to parent my son in a healthy way.

More family healing was happening too. Ann moved up in November 1984, to complete a four-year degree at a state university.

Around Christmas 1984, I wrote and illustrated a fairy-tale in a little book for Adam. I also made some puppets, and we did a puppet show together. I made him a sword and cape, and he played the role of the prince in the fairy-tale. What joy we had!

During my training at the college, I realized how I had had no opportunity to develop in my own poverty-stricken childhood, nor had I known how to help my children develop in artistic, creative ways. I was trying to add some of these things to Adam's life.

The blessings of spiritual science were spreading slowly but surely throughout my family, and not just to Richard and me.

14
Richard's Pain

When I completed the two-year training at the College in 1985, I realized that I hadn't developed enough artistically to become a Waldorf teacher.

I enrolled in the Arts Program where we painted veils with water colours. We did exercises putting on veil after veil of colour, from which forms arose. Then with our imaginations we created a picture using these forms. For example, if we saw something that looked like a castle, we would build a fairy-tale picture. To my dismay, I discovered that my imagination was blocked. I could worry with great imagination, but that was about it!

I read Grimm's fairy-tales every night, struggling to imagine the scenes. Adam and I painted them when we were together. This helped.

Meanwhile, a friend introduced me to the writing of Valentin Tomberg, a Russian Jew who had become an Anthroposophist.* Tomberg wrote about anthroposophical subjects as seen through the eyes of a soul born in the East. I related deeply to his writings. I could feel that Richard enjoyed Tomberg so much that I read him several of his early books twice.

Yet I was still struggling to understand suffering. Tomberg's writing about the difference in the concept of suffering between the East and West was very enlightening. He said that we in America are in a 'wilful pursuit of

---

* Tomberg, who died in 1973, became a Roman Catholic after the Second World War. His last books, *Meditations on the Tarot* and *Covenant of the Heart*, are written from a Catholic perspective.

absolute "positivity" by which suffering shall be eliminated.'* How true, I agreed.

A Russian's concept of suffering is the opposite; it is seen in two ways: 'Either one deserves punishment for wrong doing, or one suffers the pain of sacrificing something lower so something higher can arise.'†

Tomberg says that the Russian author Dostoyevsky's concept of suffering as presented in his *The Brothers Karamasov* truly represents Russian thinking. This concept has four parts:

every sufferer suffers for all;
every punishment can be transformed into sacrifice, into the birth pangs of a higher man;
of one individual's crime, many are guilty; and
all suffering can be experienced as the breath of Christ's spirit in human souls.‡

I was deeply moved by this concept. I realized that I had no inkling of why Richard suffered. Another realization followed quickly: Richard never complained about his suffering. Indeed, he seemed to feel it belonged to him. I had read this as self-destructive. How simplistic my thinking had been!

In my sixty-third year, I had health problems and I felt I might die. I was sitting on the couch writing about these feelings when, on an impulse, I wrote the question to Richard, 'If I die, would you meet me?'

Then I started feeling waves of agitation around me. Richard was present, and he let me know it wasn't time for me to leave. He still needed my help. He chided me that he never thought I would give up. He told me there was no one on earth except me to help him. Even after three years of

---

*Valentin Tomberg, *Early Articles*, Candeur Manuscripts, NY.
† Ibid., p. 101.
‡ Ibid., pp. 101.

daily reading to him, he was still isolated in the spiritual worlds. He had not even met his father. He also told me that his light would dim if I died, and my own light would be dimmed if I didn't remain on earth longer.

'Calm down,' I told Richard. 'I will do everything I can to stay here. And I will continue the reading until you tell me you don't need it any more.'

This communication answered my questions about the state of his consciousness. So I continued to read to him while I worked to improve my health.

To facilitate my own healing, I read and studied in depth several times an inspired book* by B. C. J. Lievegoed, M.D., a psychiatrist, educator and industrial psychologist from Holland. Its theme is man's inner development from ancient to modern times. Lievegoed developed a psychotherapy which he describes as 'biographic therapy' because its aim was 'to place the problems of the patient in the context of the biographical development of life as a whole and not look for the causes only in shocks and frustrations experienced in the patient's earliest past.'†

Lievegoed diagnoses the ills and escape routes in today's culture—anorexia nervosa, psychopathic behaviour and addictions—and describes how to heal these in new ways. These methods include artistic therapy, exercises to strengthen the will, observation exercises to bring one into the present, reading and discussion of classic literature, practising positive thinking, journal work, exercises for developing self-discipline, and the visualization of fairy-tales, myths, legends, and so on. All of these develop the soul.

After some soul-development, it's possible to create a life-style that expands into the study of spiritual knowledge, meditation and new goals in life. Gaining much insight into my own biography, I pored over this book again. I was

---

*Bernard Lievegoed, *Man on the Threshold*, Hawthorn Press, Stroud.
†Ibid., p. 14.

already doing many of these things. I added his other suggestions into my routine which greatly improved my health.

During this time, I could feel that Richard really was listening intently. I knew that these therapies would have filled the needs of his soul and spirit as they did mine. I firmly believe that I would have died during that year if I hadn't added the arts and soul exercises to my life. No wonder I had been addicted to alcohol, tobacco, coffee, and anxiety. My soul had been impoverished.

I remember thinking that Richard could have been such a remarkable person had his psychiatrist been Dr Lievegoed! My heart went out to all troubled souls who are looking for creative solutions. Throughout all the long years of trying to find help for Richard, not one solution was found. He was given drugs which only separated him from his soul.

I believe that Dr Lievegoed would have been able to find ways to enable Richard to have lived a productive life, even with his problems.

Next I turned to philosophy, because Richard had read a lot of philosophy during his search for truth. I laboured through *Riddles of Philosophy*,* a vast, erudite book that was rough going for me. I persevered through its 500 pages because it 'presented the evolution of man's consciousness revealed through the history of philosophical thought'. Because Richard had such an unerring sense for truth, I believed that he appreciated this comprehensive work.

The reading helped me to realize how little time I had spent in thought during my life. I know I wouldn't have read some of these books except for Richard. The impact of my relationship with Richard on my life was becoming filled with wonder and mystery.

---

* Rudolf Steiner, *The Riddles of Philosophy*, Anthroposophic Press, NY.

The *Riddles of Philosophy* whetted my appetite and I next read Richard *The Redemption of Thinking.** The question of this book is: can thinking lead to true spiritual knowledge of man and the universe instead of dependence on Church teachings and blind faith? The author shows how Plato's and others' spiritual views of man and the universe were lost. This vision was found again by Thomas Aquinas' intuitive insights, only to be lost again after Aquinas' death. Thinking became brain-bound and the physical world lost its connection with the spiritual world.

Then the author tells how, using scientific methods, he broke through to objective consciousness of spiritual worlds, just as we experience objectively the physical world. We can do the same if we practise daily the spiritual exercises used by the author.

I felt this book was what Richard had been looking for while on earth—a way to break through into the spiritual worlds. I felt he was eagerly receiving this knowledge. Inspired by this book, I began doing the thinking exercise again. I wondered if Richard had inspired me to read the two books about philosophy.

Hoping he could better recognize them when he was finally released from his isolation, I chose next to read him many lecture series† about the relationships of the beings in the spiritual worlds.

In my journal writing and inner working, I was inspired

---

* Rudolf Steiner, *The Redemption of Thinking,* Anthroposophic Press, NY.
† Rudolf Steiner, *The Spiritual Hierarchies; Philosophy, Cosmology and Religion; Spiritual Beings in the Heavenly Bodies and in the Kingdoms of Nature; Man and the World of the Stars,* Anthroposophic Press, NY. *The Forming of Destiny and Life after Death, Earthly Death and Cosmic Life,* Garber Communications, Blauvelt, New York. *Supersensible Influences in the History of Mankind, Planetary Spheres and Their Influence on Man's Life on Earth and in the Spiritual Worlds,* Rudolf Steiner Press, London. *The Driving Forces of Spiritual Powers in World History,* Steiner Book Center, Toronto.

to rock and sing a Russian lullaby to Richard, David and Ann as babies. I would picture them on my lap and sing to them, hugging them with much love. I knew this love flowed to them, healing them as much as it healed me. It's never too late to be a good mother!

Journal entry, 26 January 1986: 'I am beginning to see that I didn't do my karmic duty for Richard. I ran from my karma there.'

Journal entry, 20 July 1986: 'I feel Richard might write music for autistic children in the next life.'

Journal entry, 19 February 1987: 'I am seeing my children more spiritually. Ann saved my life. I wouldn't have gone into a recovery programme except for her. David has provided balance and love in the family. He could communicate both with his father and me when we divorced.'

Journal entry, 27 March 1987: 'Gifts Richard has given me: Inspiration to read to the dead and to go out into the world and try to help people like him.'

Journal entry, 2 July 1987: 'My being a mother was a crucifixion. My being a grandmother is a resurrection.'

On 11 July 1987, in meditation, I felt that Richard wanted to tell me something. He said, 'I have turned a corner and am coming back to the light. See me and everyone else in the light every day.' I realized on rereading that this was the fifth anniversary of Richard's death.

From that day forward I added to my routine the placing of everyone I prayed for in the light of Christ. I was becoming more open to Richard. It seemed as though he was working to heal others too.

Then on 6 December 1987, Richard appeared to me in a dream at the place he had died. He was lying face down in the water, and he looked like a rag doll trying to come alive. He would slightly raise his head and move his arms, then they would flop down, and he seemed dead again. This happened several times. Then he said to me: 'I'm not alive and I'm not dead. It is so dull.'

I awakened with a start. I grabbed a robe, went into the living room and picked up my journal and lit a candle. I felt so sorry for him. I was crying. I felt helpless. I wrote down the details of the dream, then put myself back into the dream and brought it to a happier conclusion. I visualized myself going into the water and bringing him out. When we reached the bank, I imagined Christ standing there. I took Richard to him and said, 'Please, Christ, heal my son. He is in such pain.'

I imagined Christ surrounding him with light. Then his Guardian Angel took him into the forest where he heard the Music of the Spheres.

I felt some relief after that. As I sat there pondering, this experience vividly brought home to me the horrible consequences of suicide. Yet I knew that the reading was giving him answers to questions of life and meaning in the universe, but Richard still had to suffer the consequences of death by his own hand. I vowed with fervour to continue my reading.

15
Some Insights on Pain and Karma

I was so moved by this experience that I started working daily in meditation with Richard and Christ. I would ask Richard and Christ to come. In my meditation of 18 January 1988, I saw Richard as a baby crawl into Christ's lap and say: 'I'm sorry I killed myself. I'll never do that again.' I was so glad to see Richard is alive with the Christ. I sensed that Richard was growing through my reading to him.

Through this experience, I started working daily with all my children as babies and me, too. We all 'sat' in Christ's lap enveloped in His love.

Meanwhile, I decided to read Richard everything I could find on karma. I thought that if he had more knowledge about his karma and how to balance it, his pain would be easier to bear. I read several such books.

While reading I began to understand more about suffering. I had learned years ago that we have a higher self and a lower self. The higher self, which we are usually unconscious of, knows our purpose and leads us to our karma, to our sufferings.

'With our ordinary consciousness we resist sorrows and suffering, but the cleverer man within us leads us towards these sufferings in defiance of our consciousness because, by overcoming them, we can strip off something.'*

Illness does the same thing. We choose our illnesses in between life and rebirth. Each illness helps one overcome a moral defect or to advance some other quality for the future.

Our higher self even plans our accidents to bring us to a

---

*Rudolf Steiner, *Reincarnation and Karma*, Anthroposophic Press, NY. *Manifestations of Karma*, Rudolf Steiner Press, London.

higher good. Richard had so many painful accidents, even catching on fire one time. Had he planned them himself? I remember his saying after his fire accident, 'I was afraid my shirt would catch on fire if I opened it one more time over that stove.' He seemed to know he would be burned.

Another thing I read is that if we are caught up in world accidents that are not our karma the spiritual world compensates us in a later life. That was such a comfort and helped dissipate more of my childhood vision of a punishing God.

I saw that karma has many aspects. Major suffering is chosen ahead; suffering is either corrective or will be compensated later. Some suffering might relate to the times, or to a nation, or to a place of our birth rather than be personal. We even might have agreed to take on world karma or to help someone else with their karma. Also, all suffering brings light. In any case, karma can be rightly understood through spiritual work.

I was coming to believe that Richard's life of unrelenting, increasing, unrelieved pain and suffering had a greater purpose than just overcoming karma. I began to feel great reverence and awe for the individuality who had been my son. I sensed that Richard's soul and spirit had accomplished much this lifetime, and that he was progressing rapidly in the spiritual worlds. What a mystery I was in!

This mystery of Richard's suffering so haunted me that I went to talk with a Christian Community priest. 'It's possible that when someone suffers that much, he is preparing to bring something new to the world,' was his suggestion. More mystery.

Personally, I was hounded by one illness after another during these years. Was I trying to overcome moral defects with these illnesses? I was terrified of dying. I had to work on that for months until I finally one day realized that it didn't matter whether I was alive, in the process of dying, or dead, as long as Christ was with me. Furthermore, I knew that Christ would never abandon me, and I sure wasn't going to walk away from Him. I was learning not to take suffering so personally and to feel a connection with Christ's suffering.

I had to face other fears—of using all of my savings on illness, of becoming too ill to work, and many more. Some days my fears were so strong that I literally had to spend an hour at a time repeating meditations for overcoming fear. All of this was working on my karma, though I didn't really understand that at the time.

During this time also I read Richard a fascinating book about the meaning of evil in our time and how to transform it.* Life in this world was making some sense through reading these books. I hoped this knowledge was as helpful to Richard as to me.

I found these books were exactly what he needed. A few months later, in early 1988, Richard appeared again in a dream, very upset.

I asked him: 'You found out that suicide didn't work, didn't you?'

'I sure did,' he answered.

Then I said: 'This is what you have to do to compensate for your committing suicide.'

He replied, appearing extremely agitated, 'It's quite enough.'

He was really disturbed. I had never seen him in such a state when alive.

The encounter with Richard was still vivid in my mind when I woke. The first thing I did was record it in my journal. Then I sat and pondered it for a long time. While pondering, I had the feeling that Richard had been given the task of working with suicides soon after they died. This seemed to cause him much pain. I wondered if it was because the deep wound of his own suicide hadn't healed,

---

* Alfred Schultze, *The Enigma of Evil*, Floris Books, Edinburgh.

and every time he met a new suicide it wrenched him deeply.

Whereas I felt compassion for Richard, I was jubilant that after only four and a half years of reading to him, he might be able to start helping other suicides!

I continued to sit there feeling great joy. Oh, the miracle of spiritual science, of learning that reading to the dead could help them! This miracle fed Richard daily.

Journal entry, 3 March 1988: 'I feel that Richard's mind is open and that he and I are helping suicides. He meets them as they cross the threshold and brings them to listen to my reading when they're able to hear. Thank you, Christ, for making this possible.'

At that time I also added people I knew who had committed suicide recently, a friend's son, and others to my reading list.

I decided to give Richard more knowledge about karma and reincarnation. It seemed to have helped him before. So I read eight more volumes of lectures on karma.*

---

*Rudolf Steiner, *Karmic Relationships*, Vols I, II, III, IV, V, VI, VII, VIII, Rudolf Steiner Press, London.

16
Richard Finds Peace

I couldn't help feeling that Richard and I had both come a long way over the years through our work together since his death. I was still amazed that he seemed able to work with others in the spiritual worlds. I wished I were more clairvoyant and could communicate with Richard at will. I wondered if he had tried to communicate with me often. Had I been unable to hear?

How far Richard had come was revealed to me on 4 July 1988, some months after the last dream, near the sixth anniversary of his death. Once more he appeared to me in a dream.

This dream was totally different from the last two dreams. Richard had moved to a new place, to a room filled with light. It was in perfect order. (Richard had been such a disorderly person.) A shelf overflowing with beautiful things and mementos from a happy, productive life adorned the four walls. When I entered the room Richard looked up at me and said joyfully, 'I can see everything from here.'

My heart filled with profound gratitude. Richard had found some peace at last and so had I.

I still continued to read to Richard, although I felt some sort of completion with his most recent past life and suicide. I didn't know where we were going from here.

In October 1988 I attended a conference on evil. This was several months after the last dream. Werner Glas, then the General Secretary of the Anthroposophical Society in the United States, said that we have to work with suicides (read to them and communicate with them). Glas said that not only are they isolated, in great despair, in the spiritual worlds, but their unspent life forces can be used by evil beings to accelerate evolution in a destructive way. If, however, we help suicides, their unspent life forces can be used for great good. I was delighted to have my and Richard's work validated.

I was beginning to learn that my reading to Richard had a far greater effect than I had ever dreamed. In great ignorance I had started the process of reading to Richard five years earlier. As my knowledge grew and intermittent contacts with Richard informed me about his changing situation, my past relationship as his mother became more and more objective, and my interest in him as a spiritual being grew. I felt that he must have been quite spiritually advanced before he had become my son to have progressed so far in such a short time after his death.

I was still somewhat baffled by his life of extreme suffering, but I knew by this time in my studies that suffering was never meaningless or random. I knew and trusted that the answer to Richard's suffering would be answered eventually.

As limited as I felt my knowledge to be, after the conference I felt strongly that my experiences with Richard should be shared.

A few weeks later, on 2 November 1988, I gave a talk on All Souls Day (a day dedicated to remembering the dead and praying for them). I told the audience about Richard and his death by suicide, and all the experiences I had had during the years of reading to him. Many people were greatly moved by my story.

I continued to read to the dead, though I knew that Richard was in a new place.

Part III

AN UNEXPECTED TURN

17
This Book is Conceived

Richard's release into a place of light in the spiritual worlds released me, too. I felt that he was in a good place, and my pain about him had been transformed into joy.

In October 1988, I had my first dream about Richard since he had moved to his new place of light. He was with me and another woman, and he was sitting between us with his arms around our shoulders. He was filled with life and talking enthusiastically. I recognized this as being one of those dreams that had a significant message, but I didn't see how it related to the past.

I have dreams on many levels, and only a few seem to be direct messages. I was delighted to see Richard so happy in this dream, but I didn't think more about it since it didn't require any action on my part. I recorded it, as usual.

My attention at that time was still on me. I continued to have one health crisis after another, and I still felt much pain about my relationships with my children.

The first dictum on a spiritual path is 'Know thyself'. It seemed that my spirit was pushing my soul and body to the wall to do this. My anthroposophical doctor told me that my high blood pressure was caused by something trying to come up from the unconscious.

In trying to heal myself during these years of trials, I kept reading or hearing two truths which I meditated on often. Firstly, Carl Jung, the noted Swiss psychiatrist, said that all neuroses are a substitute for legitimate suffering. Here was my dogged companion, suffering, again. I identified with Jung's concept. My own reservoir of pain surfaced now that Richard seemed to have found his place in the spiritual worlds. I could see that my compulsions and addictions had covered up my pain. I found that I was petrified of my feelings. However, the pain became so intense that I started going to an Al-Anon Twelve-step programme where I found a sponsor, and began to face the pain of my life. This took over three years to work through.

The other truth was from Rudolf Steiner who said, 'Illness isn't suffering, it's an opportunity to overcome an obstacle by uncovering the Christ power within.'* I repeated this concept over and over like a mantra, and kept struggling to find the obstacles causing the illnesses and to use Christ's power to overcome them.

Then I discovered in another of Steiner's books† 'Out of suffering arises learning; out of learning, knowledge. And just as in respect of much else, we may say of pain that we have grasped it only when we know it not only in itself but in what proceeds from it. As so many other things, pain too is known only by its fruits.' I meditated about this many times, comforting myself with these thoughts.

In my journal I wrote, 'Richard, our pain and suffering are bearing fruit now. Richard and I are working together on the spiritual planes. Richard and I are having an adventure together.'

Some comfort to me also during this time was something Scott Peck says in his book *The Different Drum*,‡ 'Oddly, the best measure of psycho-spiritual health is how many crises we can cram into a lifetime.' My psycho-spiritual health had to be improving by leaps and bounds! I hoped the body would follow.

Despite the illnesses, by this time I was teaching remedial reading to children at the Sacramento Waldorf School. I was

---

* Rudolf Steiner, *Festivals and Their Meanings*, Rudolf Steiner Press, London.

† Rudolf Steiner, *The Origin of Suffering, The Origin of Evil, Illness and Death*, Steiner Book Centre, North Vancouver, p. 16.

‡ Scott Peck, *The Different Drum*, Simon and Shuster, New York, p. 80.

able to establish deep rapport with the children, which was profoundly healing for me.

I also threw myself into working for the Anthro-posophical Society and participated in study groups. I continued to read to Richard and several others.

One day my friend Patricia called from San Diego to wish me a happy Valentine's Day. During the conversation Patricia said, 'My sister has been nursing a friend the past few months, who died from AIDS yesterday. Even though she knew he was dying, she is still devastated. When are you going to write a book about reading to the dead? Many people are losing loved ones to AIDS. Your book would help them.'

I knew the moment she asked that I would write a book about my experiences.

18
Can This Be True?

I started to think about the book, and made a tentative outline. I had a burning desire to try to prevent suicides. I also knew that reading spiritually inspired works to them can help them tremendously as well as be healing for the one left behind. Until then I had found it impossible to overcome Richard's suicide in my life.

I planned to end the book with Richard's moving to a place of light. However, the dream messages continued to come. From this point on, I will not mention dates for reasons that will become obvious. The sequence is exactly as it happened, only the dates have been omitted.

The next was a dream where I was living in a suite of rooms within an apartment with a young couple, new friends, whom I'd met recently. I had a baby, which was a baby from past times, but was also a baby in the present. My suite had a swinging door which opened onto the street. The husband came into our suite and formally invited the baby and me to accompany them to California. This dream remained a mystery to me for a long time; however, I sensed it was one of those message dreams.

In real life, the young woman and I became close friends. We spent much time together. She was very loving and supportive. We became rather like mother and daughter, she being the mother.

Then I had two dreams about Richard. One, he was still in bed, and I needed to awaken him to go to find a job. The other came a week later. I dreamed that he was having trouble finding work. In the dream I realized that I had been neglecting Richard lately, and promised myself to start helping him again.

What could these two dreams mean? I couldn't connect them with anything at the time. Had he finished his work with suicides? Did he need my help again? I hadn't been reading to him as faithfully since he had entered into a place of light. I felt alerted, and resumed my daily reading.

Soon after, I had a dream where a renowned spiritual teacher was leading a service of an entire spiritual community of people world-wide for Richard's sake. Everyone there was participating in singing, saying meditative verses, listening and responding to the leader. The service went on for hours. While this was happening, I saw Richard conversing with a Christian Community priest who was trying to help him understand his life in a positive way.

The priest asked Richard, 'What if your life was to provide the archetype of one who had overcome hindrances and made it possible for others to do so, too?'

I don't know what Richard's response was to the priest. When the service ended, the one who had conducted the service came to me and asked, 'How did you know we were having this service?'

'I don't know how I knew.' I answered. To myself I thought, 'Why didn't he tell me himself about it. After all, Richard was *my* son.'

I knew this dream was very significant, and I pondered over it many times. What did Richard's being an archetype mean? My spiritual teacher told me, 'Usually, an archetype is someone who does something that will help many people.' Could this be an inkling of the meaning of his suffering? Had overcoming his hindrances made it possible for others to do so? When and how? I finally gave up on that question and reviewed the rest of the dream. I didn't understand the significance of not having been told about the service. I was impressed that a whole community had been involved in helping Richard. Whatever was happening was far bigger than Richard and me. All I could do was record it and let time continue to unfold the story. Another chapter seemed to be beginning.

During this time, as my knowledge grew, I wondered what effect the voluminous reading would have in Richard's next life. Would he show an early aptitude for things spiritual? Because of the archetype dream, I wondered if we were involved in something which I was unable to bring to consciousness because of my lack of clairvoyance.

Journal entry: 'This is Richard's death date. I feel warmth and understanding between me and Richard. Hooray!'

Journal entry: 'I have spent my life trying to alleviate pain instead of listening to its message.'

Journal entry: 'How wonderful that love can reach beyond death and can heal a suicide.'

Journal entry: 'Even a suicide can be turned into a victory.'

About this time my friends had a baby, a little girl, whom I'll call Maria. I felt a deep connection with the child and offered to babysit at any time. This was their first child. The mother had had a miscarriage the year before.

I felt so close to Maria that I started doing meditative karmic exercises the day she was born, and hoped to learn what our connection was. A few days later I had the thought Maria might be Richard, but I quickly dismissed the thought as preposterous. I didn't even write it down in my journal!

Then, much to my surprise, I once again felt Richard's hovering presence. I felt his deep unrest as I had so many times before. What could this mean? He had been so happy. What had happened? I kept getting the message, 'Don't leave me now that I've returned. I need your help more than ever.' He seemed filled with anxiety.

I simply couldn't believe that he could have returned, and I dismissed it again. I continued to read to him, hoping that would calm him down. It didn't. I kept puzzling over this new development trying to make sense out of it.

In my journal I wrote:

I awoke this morning with the words 'transform hate into love.' I am becoming aware or Richard's and my present relationship. He was a searcher like me. I feel the need to be in contact with him to write the book. I am feeling that he is connected with the anthroposophical community and that our work together is community work.

I feel that Richard has been waiting for me to listen to him and get beyond the personal problems and pain we had when we were together—to get beyond the pain so we can truly bear the fruit of the pain.

I feel part of Richard's destiny was to lead me into Anthroposophy. I have to break through to him to see how we are sharing Anthroposophy now.

Richard told me he could see everything from there. Help me, Richard, I need to see everything so I can do my work. I have to let go of seeing only family ties and see all of my children in a spiritual way.

I was trying to reach him and relieve his apprehension, refusing the thought that he could be back.

The mystery continued to unfold. One morning I dreamed that Richard lay in a coffin. He sat up, climbed out and walked away. He was immaculately dressed, looked quite handsome and full of life. Then someone came and took me to the Christ. Christ was barely discernible, and we had no conversation. I didn't know why I was taken to Christ. I had taken Richard to Christ a few years earlier and asked Him to heal Richard. My overall impression of the dream was that Richard was taking on a new life. Meanwhile, Richard's presence persisted.

I wrote in my journal that day: 'Dear Christ, could these few years of reading to someone enable them to return in so short a time? I had a thought earlier about Richard and Maria, but rejected it.

'I am feeling that reading to suicides and the dead could

save them time in kamaloca and in finding Anthroposophy when they return. We could change the world quickly by reading to the dead. Especially if we could be in contact with them and work on evolution together.'

The idea of a rapid reincarnation was not foreign to me. I had met two other persons before who had reincarnated quickly. One was a young woman I met in the 70s while still living in Los Angeles. She had been a heroin addict and had become a prostitute to support the habit. She came into a recovery programme and to me for counselling. During one of our sessions, she had a flash of her former life and her dying of a heroin overdose in the 1930s. This lifetime she overcame the habit, returned to college and became a psychologist.

The other time, I was visiting a young couple who had lost a young daughter to cancer a few years earlier. Because of this tragedy, the couple changed their lives completely. The father gave up a stage career and devoted his life to educating others about the alternative treatment of cancer. They had invited me to be on a panel of people who had overcome cancer with alternative treatments.

When I arrived at their house, they told me their story. Later, they brought in a baby girl a few months old. I felt immediately that this child was the one who had died earlier and I said this to them.

Their answer was, 'Oh yes, we know she is the same soul. She came in and died to lead us into our life's work. We have her with us again!' So, I accepted that a rapid incarnation was possible.

However, I couldn't integrate yet that the new girl baby in my life could be Richard. Yet, I felt Richard's compelling presence. What could it mean? My intellect rebelled at the thought that Richard could be back. But Richard's presence was so palpable that I went back in my journal and read all of the dreams since July 1988, when Richard moved to a place of light. I had thought that was really the culmination of my experience with him. Evidently, I was wrong.

Then I began to see the picture unfold. The dream where Richard was sitting between me and another woman, talking excitedly, finally connected. It seems to me that Richard could have been sitting between me and his future mother, talking about his new life. He had his arms around both of us. He seemed to be including me in his next life, too. I knew from my study that the baby's mother would have to agree to have this soul come to her. Births aren't random events.

The next dream of me and a baby living in an apartment with the couple seemed to me to symbolize their taking on the obligation of the new baby's life. In this dream I was included in the baby's new life too. The formality with which the baby and I were invited to go with them to California gave a solemn overlay to this dream.

Then came the two dreams where Richard was looking for work and having a hard time finding it. It was during this time that the young woman had a miscarriage. I believe that Richard was displaced by the miscarriage and needed my constant support again, as I felt in the dream that I hadn't been helping him enough. Richard would have to wait in the spiritual worlds until the mother recovered enough for another pregnancy.

Next came the dream about the service for Richard. I realized the spiritual substance that had come to Richard through this long service. Strong measures would be needed to give him strength to come back so soon after so short a time. I felt I hadn't been told of the service because it wasn't for *my* son, it was for the new life of the girl baby.

Following this was the dream where Richard stepped out of his coffin and walked away. The child was born about that time. Perhaps my being led to the Christ in that dream was for me to release Richard as my son and to relate to him through the Christ.

These dreams, coupled with my intense feelings of

Richard's imperative presence, seemed to support the idea that he had returned. I knew that when we are asleep we dwell in the spiritual worlds and work with our spiritual family during the night. Rudolf Steiner says, 'We approach the dead in our dreams. Dreams are really always a previous companionship with the dead springing from our life of feeling.'* I decided to keep an open mind concerning the possibility that Richard/Maria were the same entity. I also continued to do the karmic exercises to learn more.

---

* Rudolf Steiner, *Earthly Death and Cosmic Life*, Spiritual Research Division (a division of Garber Communications, Inc.), Blauvelt, NY.

19
From Richard to Maria

My first dream about the baby girl came a few days after her birth. She had messy pants and needed me to change them. I didn't know the significance of this dream. Why would she need my help? Richard's unrest was still hovering around me, insisting he needed my help. I felt besieged and there was no one I could confide in. What was going on? I just couldn't make the switch from Richard to Maria.

Shortly afterwards I had a second dream about the child. She was naked and had urinated on the bed. She crawled into the pool of urine and would have drowned in it if I hadn't removed her.

The following morning, I sat for a couple of hours grappling with the meaning of the dream. Richard had drowned. The baby would have drowned if I hadn't rescued her. The baby's need seemed life-threatening in this dream. She seemed to be trying to get my help and attention, too. In addition, the feeling of Richard's constant presence continued. I felt both Richard and the baby wanted my help.

Finally, after five weeks of Richard's unswerving presence, I called my friend Patricia, in San Diego, the same Patricia whose question about writing the book brought it into actuality. She is clairvoyant. I asked: 'Patricia, would you check on Richard for me? I keep getting messages from two sides that he is back and won't rest until I promise him/her my continued support.'

She placed herself in meditation right then. After a few minutes, she said, 'Yes, his transformed soul and spirit have returned. You are correct in feeling that he wants your support more than ever. You are the only one on earth so far who knows who he's become. Trust your feelings.'

'Thank you, Patricia,' I sighed with relief. 'I'm not crazy after all. It's mind-boggling to be with the same entity in different bodies twice in one lifetime.'

When I put down the phone, I wrote in my journal, 'I realize that Maria needs a lot of healing because she was Richard's soul. The dreams about her messy pants and almost drowning in her urine show she needs my help. I must start thinking of Richard / Maria now and in the future and not just the past. I need to send Richard / Maria healing every day without fail.'

Oh, Christ, how it will heal me to be able to love, heal and nurture her in person when I couldn't do that when the soul was Richard. Oh, the mystery of it all. I have a new identity in relationship with Richard/Maria. We both have new identities. I am a dear family friend and love her dearly. No abysses are between us in this lifetime!'

I needed to meditate often to convince myself that Richard could be Maria. I accepted it spiritually, but I hadn't integrated it emotionally yet.

The third dream about Maria came shortly thereafter. She had messed her pants and stuck her hand in the diaper and had smeared the bowel movement all over her face. I stopped at a motel to change her. A doctor was present and planned to examine her. Here was a third dream where she needed my help, each dream more insistently than the last, and this one included a doctor. I felt these dreams connected with the feelings I had from Richard's presence, which persisted incessantly.

After this dream I surrendered. I went into meditation and promised Richard and his Guardian Angel that I would carry him in my consciousness and send her/him Christ's love and light every day. I promised to look out spiritually for Maria/Richard now, during her entire new lifetime, both while I'm still on earth and when I'm in the spiritual worlds after death.

After that meditation, I finally felt Richard's presence recede. His soul seemed in peace once more. I began to place this soul as Maria in the light every day in place of Richard, and I didn't read to him any more. My attention from now on would be on Maria.

20
O Suffering, Where Is Thy Sting?

During these unsettling weeks with Richard, I was still working through the negative feelings of my life.

I wrote in my journal: 'The agony of my life is the agony of my relationships with my children. Richard wasn't able to show love, to relate with others. I wasn't able to connect with my children. All I could do was worry about them and feel guilty and worthless because I didn't feel joy with them.

'Dear Christ, I accept my maimedness as a mother. Please heal me and my children. I can hold Richard as a baby now, and "she" is in a warm, loving space. Every day I take my family to Christ and place them in His light.'

Journal entry: 'Richard has come back through the Christ power of resurrection. Maria needs a lot of help because of her past life and suicide, and I am the only one who knows who she is. Love is such a healing force. I must take my healing and giving spiritual energy to Maria as seriously as I have my reading to Richard.'

Yet, I couldn't tell another soul about Maria. At that time I didn't know what to do with the information, so I said nothing. Meanwhile, I saw Maria at least once a week. I became part of her family. I felt deep reverence and awe to be able to play with her and show her affection. We had a wonderful time together.

One day I was sitting on the couch. She ran over, climbed up in my lap, put her arms around me and said, 'You can have a kiss and a hug.' My joy was ineffable.

One day I went to visit Maria. She was asleep. Her mother said, 'We had an astrosopher do Maria's natal chart. Would you like to listen to the tape?'

'Yes,' I answered eagerly.

As I listened to the reading, I was amazed how the astrosopher described Richard's past life so accurately. He said, 'Maria has a deep wound in her soul. She was isolated in her last lifetime. She was never able to have relationships. She hasn't had the experience of working through conflicts with others. You will have to teach her how to have relationships.'

Regarding her future, he said that this lifetime she has the potential to be able to relate. He said she has great moral strength, a tactfulness of heart, understanding boundaries and an innate social grace. She has deep Christian roots and can become a Christ figure for others.

Further, he said she has had a tremendous training in understanding truth; that she will be able to separate the essential from the non-essential. Because of this and other aspects of her chart, she can become a prominent spokesperson as the conscience of her generation.

He said she could help in a renaissance of political/cultural things and could be on a quest to speak the truth in politics. She has strong moral courage to do things.

After the tape ended, I said to her mother: 'Maria is so fortunate to have you for her mother. Your love will teach her how to have relationships with others this lifetime. She is going to be an outstanding individual.'

When I returned home, I basked in the feelings of reverence and gratitude to be associated with such a being. These feelings brought to mind another thing that Steiner had said about suffering: 'As the beauty of the pearl is born out of disease and suffering, so are knowledge, noble human nature and purified human feeling born out of suffering and pain.'* That seemed to describe Maria's soul this time perfectly. I feel that she is an archetype as the dream of the long service indicated.

At last, her natal chart seemed to me to reveal the fruit of

---

* *The Origin of Suffering*, op. cit., p. 16.

her former suffering in the glowing qualities and capacities of her soul.

The reading seemed another indication that Maria had been Richard.

I was delighted with Richard/Maria's good fortune to be with those parents. I had never met such a natural mother. She has an easy-going temperament and a giving, loving nature. I watched with awe how she handled Maria. The father is a gem, too. He has a near-genius mentality, and has two advanced degrees, one of which is in philosophy. This father can meet Maria's interest in philosophy. The two difficult books I read Richard about philosophy would be child's play for Maria's father. I have fantasies of the conversations Maria will have with her dad when those lectures I read to Richard come up from her soul when she's a seeking adult.

Maria and her parents have moved to another state now. I haven't seen her since, though we keep in touch by telephone. I send her Christmas and birthday presents. They send me pictures and videos of Maria.

I haven't dreamed about Richard since. If I never see Maria again, it's all right. I help her by sending love and by praying for her daily. From past experiences, I know if she needs more from me she'll pursue me until she gets it.

I'm not clairvoyant, but I am sensitive. I've never experienced any communication with the other dead that I've been reading to for years. I believe that the attention I gave Richard through the years created a bridge between us so we could communicate. Also, I'm convinced that the soul and spirit of Richard is living a unique destiny in which I am playing a part. I am content to let that destiny unfold.

A conversation I had with my daughter, Ann, comes to mind. It took place during Richard's increasingly difficult times. She said, 'Richard is never going to make it, is he?'

I said, 'The last chapter hasn't been written on Richard, yet.'

Little did I know at that time how prophetic those words were.

I carried the knowledge of Maria/Richard in silence for several more years. Increasingly I began to feel that I should share this experience too, that it wasn't for me alone. I mentioned it (without using names) to an anthroposophist and she said it was really soon for someone to return. Then I mentioned it to another anthroposphist and she thought it would be best to end the book without mentioning his return.

Then I confided the conflict I felt to a colleague who was helping me edit the book. She also thought it was really soon for a reincarnation. However, she was open to the possibility and she said she knew a clairvoyant who could find out if it were true. I replied, 'You can call her if you need to convince yourself. I believe it's true.'

She did call and her clairvoyant friend confirmed it, and gave my colleague several details about Maria/Richard that were true. My colleague still didn't think I should write about it.

However, my feelings grew stronger that this was not just my experience, and it needed to be shared. The dilemmas were many. I agonized over making my experiences of Richard's return public and revealing my paucity of soul when I was his mother. I knew I had to protect Maria from this knowledge until she discovered it for herself. I knew that I would have to tell her parents before the book was published. I also knew I would have to face the unbelief and derision from people on the one hand, and the curiosity of others who wouldn't understand the delicacy of the situation. But, the feeling that there is some purpose here unfolding overrode my reluctance. I have to be willing to do my part.

After months of struggle, I finally shared the information with one of my spiritual teachers. He advised me to make Richard's new incarnation known. He said it is very important that these supra-personal experiences be shared. He supported me unconditionally and wrote the Foreword.

As limited as I know my knowledge to be, I hope it will help others and bring them hope. There's nothing that can't be transformed by Christ's love.

I believe in these troubled times that rapid reincarnations could be happening more frequently. I recently read an article telling of Anne Frank's return in Sweden as Barbro Karlen. Anne Frank was the Jewish girl who hid in an attic in Holland during World War II and wrote down her experiences in a diary, which was published posthumously.

As Barbro Karlen she published her first book at age 12. She has had many other writings published since then and is well known in Sweden and Norway, and to some extent in the United States. Her books have a strong spiritual message. She spent only eight or nine years in the spiritual worlds between incarnations.

Barbro Karlen says in a report which was published in a Swedish weekly in 1973: 'I remember earlier lives the same way that one, in this life, remembers one's own childhood; it is obvious and easy. Since the age of two I have known of my life as Anne Frank. But I have nothing with which to prove this. Whoever believes me may do just that, and whoever takes reincarnation to be a lie can hold to that.'*

Richard was gone about the same length of time between incarnations as Anne Frank. Will the experience of his listening to over two thousand lectures start surfacing early in Maria's life? Will she recognize me when she gets older and feel the deep spiritual bond we have? Will we work together again in the future? I hope so, because I feel that she has helped me infinitely more than I have helped her.

I continue to work on transforming negative thoughts, attitudes and feelings. I've come to a peace and acceptance

---

*Christoph Rau, 'Barbro Karlen und Anne Frank', *Das Goetheanum, Wochenschrift für Anthroposophie*, Dornach, Switzerland.

regarding suffering and its meaning. Maria's natal chart and present life are living proof to me of the fruits of her suffering. As for myself, in my journal on 20 July 1991, I wrote, 'I realize that I chose my own suffering in this lifetime, and I'm learning to see suffering as a way to cognition, and not to passively give in to it. To overcome suffering, I have learned not to take it so personally, to try to read its message, and to trust that it is accomplishing something for myself and maybe for others.'

I believe Richard/Maria has returned with a gift for humanity. I eagerly look forward to what it might be.

My relationships with my children are greatly healed. Ann finished college, married and moved out of state. She has given me a precious granddaughter. David has started the process of 'Know thyself'. My grandson, Adam, is in his teens now, and doesn't have much time for grandmothers. However, we both cherish the wonderful times we've had together.

I celebrated my seventy-second birthday yesterday, and life is sweet.

I still don't know why we all had to experience my not being able to bond with my children, but I feel it was what our souls needed to experience for our growth.

Finally, I can trust Christ; I can trust myself; I can trust life itself.

I know that I can probably see only one thousandth, if that, of the whole picture. I know that my understanding of the events will change as my knowledge grows, or if new incidents occur. I feel confident that I am doing what this soul asked of me because Richard has not contacted me since I promised him my continued support shortly after Maria's birth; nor have I had any dreams about Maria needing my help. If anything more is needed from me, I will know.

I want to mention one last book, *Beyond the Darkness*.* This

---

* Angie Fenimore, *Beyond the Darkness*, Bantam Books, New York.

is the story of a near-death experience of Angie Fenimore who tried to commit suicide. She describes graphically the hell she discovered when she took her own life—a dark place filled with despair and lost souls. The spirit of God showed her what the consequences of her death would be for her children and all the people she was destined to meet. She chose to come back and take up her responsibilities. She is the first one I know of to write a personal experience of a suicide. I am grateful to her for her courage, which will enlighten many and, I hope, prevent more suicides.

The final thing I want to share is a verse by Michael Bauer that embodies how I think of Maria/Richard, myself and every other human being on earth or in the spiritual worlds:

> To us it is given
> At no stage ever to rest.
> They live, they strive the active
> Human beings from life unto life
> As plants grow from springtime
> To springtime ever rising,
> Through error upward to truth
> Through fetters upward to freedom
> Through illness and death
> Upward to beauty, to health and to life.*

---

* Reproduced in Rudolf Steiner, *Truth Wrought Words*, Anthroposophic Press, Spring Valley, NY.

Appendix I
One Way To Read To the Dead

I think it is important to still the mind and ask Christ's protection while reading to the dead. I light a candle, but it isn't necessary.

Then I say a prayer to the Guardian Angels of each one in the following way:

Spirit of their souls,
Effective guardians
May your wings convey
My soul's petitioning love
To those humans in the spheres
Entrusted to your care.
So, that, united with your power,
My love may radiate helpfully
To the souls it seeks in love.

Then I say another verse:

I look to you in the spirit world
In which you are.
May my love mitigate your heat.
May my love mitigate your cold.
May it come through to you and help you
To find the way
From the spirit's darkness
To the spirit's light.

Or, if you prefer, you can make up your own verse or prayer by simply saying: 'Guardian Angels of ......, please take my love and this reading to their souls.

I feel it's important to picture each one lovingly, bringing to mind an occasion where the two of you were happy together, and to try to picture them while reading.

Then read what you've chosen. The material must be spiritually inspired, e.g., the New Testament (especially the Gospel of St John), all of Ralph Waldo Emerson's work, the *Bhagavadgita*, biographies of saints. I chose Rudolf Steiner's work because he has given the most comprehensive truth about the cosmos and human beings and their connections and purpose.

I usually read a chapter a day. After I finished I would say goodbye and blow out the candle.

To be able to connect with the dead, it is necessary to feel deep love for them.

I believe if you continue to read for months or years you may become sensitive to their presence. They may even inspire you what to read to them!

If you don't feel their presence, they are still being helped immensely by your love and attention. The reading is spiritual food to them, the only food that matters after death. They can't feed themselves in the spiritual worlds, and need our help.

Happy reading. I would be interested to hear about your experiences of reading to the dead.

Appendix II
Suggestions on Communicating with the Dead

I learned in my reading that the best time to communicate with the dead is just before we fall asleep. The best time for receiving communications from them is as we awake in the morning.

One must train one's consciousness. Before going to sleep, imagine your loved one with his/her Angel standing before you and talk with them; tell them you love them and other intimate things you might want to share. Then ask them questions you need answered. I also ask my Guardian Angel to work with their Guardian Angel.

I found that many of my communications were in dreams right before awaking. I would write these dreams in my journal immediately before they slipped from consciousness.

During the day I also placed myself in a meditative state by saying a prayer or verse and writing questions in my journal. Sometimes I was able to sense Richard's presence and write his communications.

If one really wants to do this, it takes constant commitment, practice and patience. One must give up all expectations and be willing to let the Angels lead the way. Our personal desires must become higher desires to learn the karmic connections between us and how we can work together now—with them in the spiritual worlds and we on earth.

Rudolf Steiner says it's absolutely necessary for us now and in the future to learn to be in contact with the spiritual worlds, with humans who are there and other spiritual beings, to bring our human evolution to its goal. We are so enmeshed in the thoughts that only the material world is real that we can't recognize spiritual guidance easily. We need their super-knowledge to guide us.

I work at this daily. I look over my day every evening to see if I can recognize when I was helped by the dead or the Angels. Sometimes it's clear, and other times I don't realize until later. I'm sure I miss recognizing many communications.

We in America have the habit of demanding instant results. This attitude will prevent our success. Cultivating new thoughts and habits over the years will bring results in many ways. These thoughts and habits carry over into our life after death and enable us to find our way in the spiritual worlds. Our sojourns on earth are but an instant in comparison to the time we spend in the spiritual worlds.

Appendix III
Exercises to Learn about Karmic Relationships

In Rudolf Steiner's *Karmic Relationships,* Vol. II,* he gives a karmic exercise which should take place over a three-day period, culminating on the fourth day with an insight into the cause in a past life of a present-day experience. He cautions, and it has been my experience, that one has to practise this exercise many times before getting the desired results. He asks one not to give up in discouragement, advising that the gaining of spiritual knowledge about one's past life requires constant soul development and PATIENCE, PATIENCE, PATIENCE.

I had tried this exercise many times before over the years with no results, but when I did the exercise at the birth of the baby I received the information the first time. The exercise is as follows.

If, for example, a dear friend of yours hurts you in some way which surprises you, and you'd like to learn what caused his/her behaviour, the first step is to quiet your mind and visualize as vividly as possible the entire scene as it happened in great detail—the tone of voice, the body language, the place in great detail, the inner feelings you were experiencing at the time. If you accomplish the visualization strongly enough, during the night that follows your soul will work on the picture. That is the first day.

On the second day, pay attention to your feelings and continue to visualize the picture while in a meditative mood. Maybe the picture has added dimensions to it now.

---

* Rudolf Steiner, *Karmic Relationships*, Vol. II, Rudolf Steiner, Press, London.

Pay attention to any changes, and to your feelings during that day. During the night the soul works on the picture further.

On the third day you may awaken with a dream which further changes the picture and has many other pictures with it. You may get the feeling that the scene with your friend didn't actually come through him or her, but that spiritual beings brought you the experience through the friend. Then comes the third night.

On the morning after the third day, you may wake up with a picture where you can't move, you feel paralysed. But if you let the picture speak to you, it will show you an event in your past life which caused the experience you had with your friend.

In my experience with the baby, I felt so connected with the child the moment I held her in my arms that I went home and visualized myself holding her dressed in a little hat and wrapped tightly in a blanket, sound asleep. I visualized the hospital sounds, the hospital room, the parents and our conversation, and my feelings while holding the child.

By the time the three days turned into the fourth day, I was inundated with the feeling that this child had been Richard. But, my intellect couldn't accept it at the time. I brushed it aside and continued to do the exercise again, adding this time a second exercise of visualizing myself holding Richard when he was a baby. The feelings grew daily in intensity that Richard was the baby girl and that his soul would give me no rest until I accepted this—because he wanted me to help him now in his new incarnation and let the Richard incarnation go. When I finally did let Richard go and turn my attention to the new baby, the intense feelings subsided and I haven't heard from Richard since.

I've done this exercise many times over the years, but this is the first time I got such clearly defined results. I feel the other times I did the exercise strengthened my soul so I could receive this vital information at the baby's birth.

Gaining spiritual insight is a constant occupation and requires patience and perseverance. Wanting quick results retards progress. My experience with Richard and the spiritual growth that came to both of us has given me the patience of Job. For me, gaining spiritual knowledge is the only meaningful pursuit.

Afterword

Since the beginning of the century, we have lived in an age when every aspect of life is being re-examined. The conventions and traditions of the past have fallen away and no longer guide the human soul. We appear to be adrift on a raft on the high seas, buffeted by storms and winds, unable to find an anchorage. Many will no doubt feel that this is an excruciating experience and consider it cruel and totally futile. Hopelessness was voiced at the beginning of the century when Nietzsche maintained 'God is dead.' This cry of anguish still resounds powerfully through the souls of many today when nihilism and atheism are rife.

On the other side of the spectrum we find various forms of rigid fundamentalism claiming that they alone have the truth, often represented in a militant and dogmatic way.

Between these two extremes every shade of 'New Age' practice has developed with promises of easy self-enhancement in order to attain blessedness and peace of mind.

Can a golden mean be found? Is it possible, in full consciousness, through one's own inner efforts to open the eye of the spirit that is dormant in each one of us? Can one build a wholesome, harmonious, soul-bridge with those who have passed on? Is it possible to receive impulses and messages, without the intervention of clairvoyants or channellers, from those who have died?

During the first quarter of the century, Rudolf Steiner (1861–1925), the Austrian philosopher, educator and spiritual seer, indicated a disciplined path of spiritual development through Imagination, Inspiration and Intuition, by means of which the questing soul can gradually grow and attain a consciousness of spiritual realms.

This book by Doré Deverell shows in a most dramatic way how the discovery of Steiner's work marked a turning-point in the exceedingly troublesome life that she had led until then.

This is the poignant story of a young woman, mother of three, living with an engineer husband who had withdrawn from the tribulations of the family, residing in affluent parts of southern California. Outwardly, it would seem that she has everything, and is able to indulge, at least to begin with, in a free-flowing hedonistic life. She had a severe drinking problem, which she overcame. And she battled with cancer, which she has been able to heal by way of non-allopathic medicines and diet. (Incidentally she has described this remarkable cure in her book *How I Healed My Cancer Holistically.*)

She was confronted by harsh blows of fate and showed the most remarkable fortitude and perseverance in seeking answers to the riddles of her life. Richard, her first born, was far from normal, and saddled with a variety of emotional and mental problems. Nevertheless, he was remarkably gifted, both academically and musically, but a loner and misfit in society. The ultimate blow came when Richard committed suicide as a young man.

It is in this condition of utter despair that Doré found the work of Rudolf Steiner, who not only threw light on the riddle of suicide but outlined a method of daily readings to one who has died. This book testifies in an astonishing way to how real and effective such a practice, carried out with absolute regularity and devotion, can be.

Furthermore, Rudolf Steiner's work, named Anthroposophy or spiritual science, is based on the living concepts of karma and reincarnation. The question arose: can a soul who has died as a result of a self-inflicted death reincarnate? Can it find a new body for a future existence on earth? What would be the interval in such a case, between death and rebirth?

Doré Deverell, in the last portion of her book, reveals what she has experienced in this regard. It is a personal testimony, free from sentimentality and sensationalism — she tells her story in a straightforward, clear manner. It makes her saga all the more convincing. It was only after having completed her manuscript that Doré came across the reference to Anne Frank who is, according to her own testimony, re-embodied as a woman in Sweden, and lives there today, conscious of her tragic past.

I feel that this book can help those who are searching for a soul-spiritual element in their lives, where the reality of the healing presence of the Christ becomes a profound, personal experience rather than — as is often the case today — an empty belief. This book is a testimony full of hope that opens new vistas of supersensible reality, and builds a bridge between the living and the dead in the light of reincarnation and karma.

R. M. Querido, Ll.D.*
3 February 1995

---

* Author, *Questions and Answers about Reincarnation and Karma* (Rudolf Steiner College, California), and *The Golden Age of Chartres* (Floris Books, Edinburgh).

ALSO FROM CLAIRVIEW

AND THE WOLVES HOWLED
Fragments of two lifetimes
Barbro Karlén

'An extraordinary book ... deserves to be taken seriously.'
—*International Herald Tribune.*.

'... A very thought-provoking read! Whether or not she was really Anne Frank in another life, I do not doubt Karlén's sincerity.'
—Rabbi Yonassan Gershom, author of *Beyond the Ashes* and *From Ashes to Healing.*

For as long as she can remember, Barbro Karlén has harboured terrible memories of a previous existence on earth as the Jewish girl Anne Frank, author of the famous *Diary*. Until recently, she had kept this knowledge private. Now, prompted by a series of events which culminated in a struggle for her survival, she is ready to tell her amazing story.

And the Wolves Howled is the autobiography of Barbro Karlén, from her early fame as a bestselling child literary sensation in her native Sweden, to her years as a policewoman and a successful dressage rider. But this is no ordinary life history. As the victim of discrimination, personal vendettas, media assassination, libel and attempted murder, Karlén is forced to fight for her very being. In the dramatic conclusion to her living nightmare, she is shown the karmic background to these events. She glimpses fragments of her former life, and begins to understand how forces of destiny reach over from the past into the present. With this knowledge she is finally free to be herself...

£10.95; 272pp (8 b/w plates); ISBN 1 902636 18 X

PSYCHIC WARRIOR
The true story of the CIA's paranormal espionage
programme
David Morehouse

When David Morehouse—a much decorated army officer—was
hit by a stray bullet, he began to be plagued with visions and
uncontrolled out-of-body experiences. As a consequence, he was
recruited as a psychic spy for STARGATE, a highly-classified
programme of espionage instigated by the CIA and the US
Defence Department. Trained to develop spiritual, clairvoyant
capacities, he became one of a select band of 'remote viewers' in
pursuit of previously unattainable political and military secrets.

When Morehouse discovered that the next step in the top-
secret programme was 'remote influencing'—turning 'viewers'
like himself into deadly weapons—he rebelled. In his efforts to
expose the programme, he and his family endured the full force
of the US intelligence community's attempts to silence him. As
the multi-million-dollar STARGATE scandal was exposed to the
world, Morehouse himself became the enemy of the secret services...

In *Psychic Warrior*, one of STARGATE's 'viewers' finally reveals
the extraordinary truth of this secret operation.

£9.95; 280pp (8 b/w plates); ISBN 1 902636 20 1

MY DESCENT INTO DEATH
and the message of love which brought me back
Howard Storm

'For twenty years, I have been listening to and reading innumerable accounts of near-death experiences, but I have rarely encountered one as powerful as Howard Storm's' — Dr Kenneth Ring, author of *Lessons from the Light.*

'... I consider Howard Storm's near death experience one of the greatest that I am aware of ... I highly recommend this book.' — George Ritchie, author of *Return from Tomorrow* and *Ordered to Return.*

For years Howard Storm lived the American dream. He had a fine home, a family, and a successful career as an art professor and painter. Then, without warning, he found himself in hospital in excruciating pain, awaiting an emergency operation. He realized with horror that his death was a real possibility.

Storm was totally unprepared for what was to happen next. He found himself out of his body, staring at his own physical form. But this was no hallucination; he was fully aware and felt more alive than ever before. In his spirit form, Storm was drawn into fearsome realms of darkness and death, where he experienced the terrible consequences of a life of selfishness and materialism. However, his journey also took him into regions of light where he conversed with angelic beings and the Lord of Light Himself, who sent him back to earth with a message of love.

My Descent into Death is Howard Storm's full story: from his near death experience in Paris to his full recovery back home in the United States, and the subsequent transformation of his life. Storm also communicates what he learned in his conversations with heavenly spiritual beings, revealing how the world will be in the future, the real meaning of life, what happens when we die, the role of angels, and much more. What he has to say will challenge those who believe that human awareness ends with death.

£8.95; 184pp (8 b/w plates); 1 902636 16 3

SEVEN STEPS TO ETERNITY
The true story of one man's journey into the afterlife
as told to 'psychic surgeon' Stephen Turoff

'I died in the Battle of the Somme...' These were the astonishing
first words spoken to clairvoyant and healer Stephen Turoff by
the soul of James Legett, a soldier who was killed in the First
World War. For two years, the world famous 'psychic surgeon'
communicated with the soldier's soul, and in the process wrote
down his remarkable story; not the tale of Legett's tragically short
life on the physical plane, but of his death on a battlefield in
France and his soul's subsequent journey into the afterlife.

Although he works with many discarnate spirits in his clinic,
the dyslexic Turoff was initially reluctant to undertake the task of
writing a book. But he was persuaded by the boisterous and
genial soul of the dead man. Their literary collaboration involved
an unusual method: Legett presented spiritual pictures to Turoff,
who with clairvoyant perception interpreted them into words.
The result is this enlightening testimony of life beyond the illu-
sion of death, filled with insight, spiritual wisdom and delightful
humour. It is written to show that we are all eternal; there is no
death ... only change.

'One of the best books of this genre to cross my desk in some time;
its easy style will be of equal appeal to experienced readers and
newcomers to spiritual matters alike.' — *Psychic News*

£8.95; 192pp; 1 902636 17 1